NEW DIRECTIONS FOR ADULT AND CONTINUING EDUCATION

Ralph G. Brockett, *University of Tennessee, Knoxville*
EDITOR-IN-CHIEF

Alan B. Knox, *University of Wisconsin, Madison*
CONSULTING EDITOR

Mistakes Made and Lessons Learned: Overcoming Obstacles to Successful Program Planning

Thomas J. Sork
University of British Columbia

EDITOR

Number 49, Spring 1991

JOSSEY-BASS INC., PUBLISHERS
San Francisco

MISTAKES MADE AND LESSONS LEARNED:
OVERCOMING OBSTACLES TO SUCCESSFUL PROGRAM PLANNING
Thomas J. Sork (ed.)
New Directions for Adult and Continuing Education, no. 49
Ralph G. Brockett, Editor-in-Chief
Alan B. Knox, Consulting Editor

Microfilm copies of issues and articles are available in 16mm and 35mm,
as well as microfiche in 105mm, through University Microfilms Inc., 300
North Zeeb Road, Ann Arbor, Michigan 48106.

LC 85-644750   ISSN 0195-2242   ISBN 1-55542-783-9

NEW DIRECTIONS FOR ADULT AND CONTINUING EDUCATION is part of The
Jossey-Bass Higher and Adult Education Series and is published quarterly
by Jossey-Bass Inc., Publishers (publication number USPS 493-930). Sec-
ond-class postage paid at San Francisco, California, and at additional
mailing offices. Postmaster: Send address changes to Jossey-Bass Inc.,
Publishers, 350 Sansome Street, San Francisco, California 94104.

EDITORIAL CORRESPONDENCE should be sent to the Editor-in-Chief,
Ralph G. Brockett, Dept. of Technological and Adult Education, University
of Tennessee, 402 Claxton Addition, Knoxville, Tennessee 37996-3400.

Cover photograph by Wernher Krutein/PHOTOVAULT © 1990.

Printed on acid-free paper in the United States of America.

CONTENTS

EDITOR'S NOTES

About fifteen years ago when I was an administrator in a university continuing education office, I noticed an interesting behavior pattern among those of us who were responsible for planning and implementing programs. Every time a program "failed," we would make a note in its folder about not offering it again and then place the folder in a special section of our filing system where it was effectively "buried." If anyone ever asked about a failed program, the person responsible for that program either would become defensive or would skillfully shift the conversation to another topic. In short, we had tacitly agreed not to disturb "the dead" in our cemetery of failed programs.

Since I was concerned about the effectiveness and efficiency of our unit, I felt we were missing a good opportunity to improve our programming. The press of other matters prevented me from doing much about it at the time, but later I wrote a brief article in which I suggested that those involved in adult and continuing education could learn how to improve the design and delivery of programs if they carefully analyzed program failures, just as physicians use postmortem examinations to discover why people die unexpectedly. Although I have since had second thoughts about the analogy (because, for some, discussing "death" is taboo), I have an unwavering belief in the utility of analyzing our educational failures to discover why they occurred and ultimately to inform our practice so that the proportion and frequency of failures can be reduced. This volume focuses on the lessons we can learn from the mistakes that we and others make as we design and deliver educational programs for adult learners.

The first chapter is devoted to identifying various types of failures in adult and continuing education, to reviewing the literature on program failure, and to emphasizing the importance of analyzing failures in order to uncover their causes and consequences.

In Chapter Two, Christine H. Lewis and Catherine C. Dunlop report the results of a research study in which practitioners in a variety of provider agencies were asked to identify "highly successful" and "highly unsuccessful" programs, to explain why they considered these programs to be successful or unsuccessful, and to speculate on the factors that accounted for success or lack of success.

Chapter Three focuses on the constant challenge of getting those for whom a program is designed to attend. Alan L. Hanson, like many of us, has faced the unpleasant task of canceling a program due to insufficient enrollment. Based on his own research and experience in continuing professional education, he discusses the consequences of this type of program failure, the decisions made in the planning process that have important implications for participation, and techniques that can be used to discover why those you hoped would attend decided to do something else instead.

NEW DIRECTIONS FOR ADULT AND CONTINUING EDUCATION, no. 49, Spring 1991 © Jossey-Bass Inc., Publishers   1

Most of us, as providers, are disappointed when learners or presenters openly express dissatisfaction with a continuing education program. In Chapter Four, Robert G. Simerly discusses the ten most common negative reactions and proposes a set of guidelines to improve the likelihood that a program will be satisfying.

As educators, we are presumably concerned with designing experiences that will promote learning. We intervene in the natural process of learning in order to bring about deliberate changes in people's capabilities. When participants in our programs do not change in the way that we intended, we and often others are disappointed. In Chapter Five, P. Bailey Allard shares her observations about what often prevents the desired learning from occurring and what we can do as planners to increase the chances that our programs will produce the changes in human capabilities that they are intended to produce. Her anecdotes should be familiar to many experienced teachers and trainers of adults; her suggestions should be useful reminders for the experienced and required reading for the novice.

A change in capability does not always lead to a change in performance. In Chapter Six, Richard W. Kemerer discusses factors that prevent the application of new capabilities when the learners return to their "natural" environment. He argues that unclear or unreasonable expectations, programs that have little relationship to the practice setting, and poorly designed reward structures account for many problems in applying what is learned. He offers strategies for increasing transfer of learning.

As several of the authors point out, acknowledging and discussing failures is not a popular activity. Even though failure is a natural part of the work that we do, we don't feel good when it happens. In Chapter Seven, Helen H. Mills looks at the emotional impact of failure and suggests more than a dozen ways of coping with it.

In the final chapter, I discuss how what is learned from a careful analysis of our mistakes can become a powerful tool that, if broadly applied, should reduce the incidence of the types of failure of greatest concern in adult and continuing education.

I would like to take this opportunity to thank the people who contributed to this volume. They all took a bit of a risk in associating themselves with a book focused largely on failure. Each person who participated in the project accepted the task willingly, took the work seriously, and produced a manuscript in a timely fashion. Thanks also go to Ralph G. Brockett, series editor, for his encouragement and suggestions throughout the project. I hope this effort to bring together in one volume a variety of perspectives on the mistakes that we make will ease the minds of those who think their failures are unique and that it will encourage more frequent and systematic efforts to turn unfortunate events into useful lessons.

Thomas J. Sork
Editor

Thomas J. Sork is associate professor of adult education at the University of British Columbia.

Making mistakes in the design and delivery of programs is inevitable, but learning from those mistakes requires deliberate reflection and systematic analysis.

Learning About Planning from Success and Failure

Thomas J. Sork

Planning education and training programs for adults is a complex decision-making process. When we set out to plan an educational event we usually do so with the intention of changing human capabilities in some way. This change may be desired by those who will participate in the program, by a planner, by an employer, by the government, by a professional organization, or by any of a wide range of stakeholders. As planning begins, the change may be well defined, ill defined, or somewhere in between. Someone may have a clear strategy in mind for bringing about the change, or no one may have the foggiest notion of where to start. Resources to bring about the change may be readily available or nonexistent. Potential participants may be highly motivated, highly skilled learners who will jump at the chance to participate, or they may be resentful of any effort to change them and refuse to participate either physically or intellectually. The climate may be conducive to participatory planning, reflective decision making, and learner-oriented designs or it may be autocratic and hierarchical and allow only teacher-oriented designs. It should surprise no one, then, that sometimes our efforts to change human capabilities are successful, sometimes they are not, and sometimes they are a little bit of both.

Success is wonderful. It gives us a sense of accomplishment, it builds our self-esteem, we are rewarded for it, and it is valued in society. A great deal can be learned about good educational planning by reflecting on our successes. Understanding which strategies account for success allows us to build a repertoire of skills that we can continually expand and refine. But focusing exclusively on success ignores the potent learning opportunities

NEW DIRECTIONS FOR ADULT AND CONTINUING EDUCATION, no. 49, Spring 1991 © Jossey-Bass Inc., Publishers

afforded by failure. If we are doing our jobs as educational providers well, then the occasional failure is inevitable. Although I know of no studies done on educational planners reputed to be "highly successful," I suspect that one characteristic they share is an uncommon willingness to take risks. And wherever there is risk-taking behavior, there is failure. As Strother and Klus (1982) observe: "One difference . . . between the successful and the unsuccessful planner lies in the ability to contend with risk and uncertainty. Contending with risk and uncertainty does not imply avoidance of either. Some very successful planners have a significant number of failures simply because they allocate a portion of their effort and resources to innovative experiments and count on a favorable payoff ratio of successes over failures. And even their failures are instructive" (p. 69).

Accepting the inevitability of occasional failure is difficult in a society that values achievement and success. But regarding failure as a wonderful opportunity to learn about and improve the work that we do may encourage more systematic exploration of the reasons for and consequences of failure in adult and continuing education.

Learning from the Failures of Others

Only a few have had the nerve to report publicly on failures they have experienced in the design and delivery of adult education programs and on what they learned as a result. Smith (1974, 1975) provided two brief case studies of programs that were canceled because of insufficient enrollments. The first program was entitled "Midlife Alternatives for Over-Forty Males." Smith provided readers with brochure copy and information on how the program was promoted, then speculated on the likely reasons why the program failed, including overpricing, an exclusive focus on males, a negative or punitive description, and untimeliness. The second program was a travel study seminar to Puerto Rico. Again, Smith provided excerpts from the promotional materials and background information on the origin of the program idea, then used a series of questions to challenge readers to conduct their own analysis of why it failed. In a follow-up article, Lacy and Smith (1976) reported on how their analysis of the "Midlife Alternatives" failure led to a revised and highly successful offering a year and a half later.

Lewis and Fockler (1976) reported on a sales training program that "bombed" in a "dry run." Their analysis led them to conclude that the design had been based on needs perceived by training managers rather than on the needs of the sales representatives for whom the program was designed. They described in detail how they went about redesigning the program so that it was relevant to the needs of the intended participants.

Downs, Holt, and Taylor (1985) described the audit of a leisure-program failure—a camp for older adults that attracted only two registrants. The auditing process involved sending questionnaires to three groups of people: those who had requested more information about the camp but did not register, those who did register, and those who had been promoting the camp through presentations to seniors groups. Results of the analysis led to the conclusion that there were problems with the time the camp was offered, its length, and proposed age groupings. The audit process also revealed inconsistencies between a needs assessment that was completed as part of the planning process and observations made by the three groups about the relevance and desirability of the final program design.

Hanson (1982) reported on a continuing education program for pharmacists that was also canceled due to insufficient enrollment, and he described the steps he took to determine why the program was not attractive. Through a detailed survey, he discovered several program characteristics that needed to be changed, including the time of year it was offered, the content, and the location.

These articles are good examples of how the experiences of failure and the insights gained from them can lead to success. Unfortunately, there are only a few of such carefully analyzed failures that are relevant to adult and continuing education.

Learning from Our Own Failures

Learning from published reports of the failures of others is useful, but our own failures provide even more relevant information because the factors that best explain them may be specific to our own setting. Several frameworks have been published to assist those who wish to analyze their programs that fail. In a 1981 article, I proposed that the idea behind the postmortem examination in medicine could be applied to adult and continuing education. I identified three types of program failures, a set of eight questions that could provide structure for the audit, and several tips for using the procedure.

Building on this work, Martin-Lindgren and Varcoe (1986) proposed a fourth type of failure—programs that do not achieve expected changes in behavior and practice—and they suggested a set of steps and provided a form that could be used to conduct a postmortem analysis.

Holt, Downs, and Taylor (1986) described how concepts and principles from systems analysis can be applied to program failure in organizations. They observed that "the purpose of failure analysis of educational programs is not to find individual scapegoats but is instead to find weak points in the flow of information and management of responsibilities in a planning system" (p. 108).

Sork, Kalef, and Worsfold (1987) developed a manual for conducting postmortem audits of four types of education and training program failures. They emphasized the importance of understanding the monetary and nonmonetary costs of failures as well as the reasons for failure. Their approach can be used to analyze single or multiple program failures, and it includes worksheets, summary forms, and other aids to guide the analyst or audit committee through the process.

Each of these approaches may be useful depending on the context in which the failure occurs and the energy and commitment that accompanies the desire to understand the failure. Marshaling the commitment and energy required to look carefully at failures is not easy given the pressures of day-to-day responsibilities and the priority that is naturally given to current and future programs. Rather than viewing the time and energy needed to do the analysis as a cost, providers should regard it as an investment toward the success of future programs.

In order to begin the process of learning from our failures, we must first agree on what we mean by failure and why we are concerned about each type of failure. How do we know that a failure has occurred? What indicators do we look for when we are trying to decide which programs are successes and which are failures? And why might it be important that we concern ourselves with more than one kind of failure?

Indicators of Planning and Program Failures

Reports of program failures found in the literature reflect a primary concern with ensuring adequate numbers of registrants in programs, but it seems a bit shortsighted to be exclusively concerned with enrollments. Insufficient enrollments indicate that the planning process may be flawed, but there are other indicators that we should also consider. The following paragraphs describe five indicators that suggest mistakes have been made in the design or delivery of programs.

Aborted Planning. When resources such as staff time, travel costs to attend meetings, telephone expenses, and so on are allocated to the planning of a program but the task is never completed, we may have evidence of a planning failure.

It is only reasonable to expect that some resources must be devoted to exploring ideas for programs sufficiently to make an informed decision about whether or not to proceed with planning. Houle (1972) includes the following as the second element in his planning model: "A decision is made to proceed." This suggests that there is a natural decision point early in the planning process when a choice is made about whether to devote additional resources to planning, with the expectation that a complete program design will result, or to cease further planning. Aborted planning occurs when the process ceases after that initial decision to proceed has been made. Determining where in the planning process it is reasonable to make the decision to proceed is a task best left to each provider organization, since only they understand the financial and other implications of allocating resources to planning activities that do not produce a program.

Aborted planning is a problem because each case represents a waste of valuable resources that could have been put to better use. The time of staff, the costs of travel and communications, and other expenses should be applied to programs that will have some benefit for the provider and participants. If a significant proportion of resources is allocated to aborted planning efforts, then the efficiency of the provider suffers and fewer programs are available to adult learners.

Insufficient Enrollment. The most obvious manifestation of insufficient enrollment is when a program that has been promoted or marketed is canceled before it is implemented. A decision to cancel a program is often justified on financial grounds. Fees for programs are often calculated on the assumption that a specified minimum number of people will register. If registrations fall short of this minimum, then the expenses of offering the program will be greater than the revenue generated. Unless there are good reasons for operating the program at a loss—and in many cases there are good reasons for doing so—the program is canceled and any fees paid are refunded. Even if participants are not paying fees, as might be the case in a voluntary inservice training program, the expected benefits of offering the program to only a few people may not be considered sufficient to justify the costs.

Insufficient enrollment may lead to program cancellation for nonfinancial reasons as well. If a key part of the instructional design includes methods that require a critical mass of participants, then the program may be canceled if that critical mass is not achieved. An example is group role play in which half the participants are part of the role play and the other half observe and analyze what happens. It might be possible to use an equally effective alternative method with a smaller group, but if the activity is considered essential to the success of the program, then cancellation is a responsible alternative.

Program cancellation should be a concern because of (1) the financial implications of allocating resources to design and market programs that produce no monetary or nonmonetary benefits and (2) the nonmonetary costs to the provider organization, such as disappointed registrants and instructors and a tarnished institutional image. Chapter Three focuses on the problem of insufficient enrollment.

Negative Reactions. It is reasonable to expect some negative reaction to every program; there always seems to be someone whose expectations have not been fulfilled or who is upset or offended by something that did or did not happen. The negative reactions that are evidence of a program failure are those that go beyond this normal occurrence.

Negative reactions are expressed in many ways, including verbally, through body language, through obstructive or distracting behavior, and by participants "voting with their feet." We often invite participants to express their reactions to our programs by giving them evaluation forms that ask specific questions about their satisfaction with the instructor, facilities, methods used, degree of social interaction, and other components. Even when we don't invite reactions, we may get them through candid comments directed at instructors or program administrators, through "delegations" of participants who represent the larger group, and through letters sent to program administrators or instructors following the program. Sometimes the comments are quite specific about what element of the program was liked or disliked; other times the comments are so vague or global that we have no idea what provoked the reaction.

Dropping out can be another form of negative reaction to programs, but there are several forms of dropout that must be differentiated. First is "normal attrition" in which participants do not wish to leave the program but do so because of illness, changed obligations, time pressures, and so on. The extent of dropout that is considered normal may vary substantially from one type of provider or agency to another. As long as dropout rates do not exceed this normal level, then no program failure has occurred. Second is "positive dropout" in which participants leave the program before its completion because "they got what they came for." Their departure from the program may be mistakenly interpreted as a negative reaction, but if their expectations are fulfilled, it is difficult to argue that the program has failed. Third is "negative dropout" in which participants leave the program because they are dissatisfied with all or part of it. Distinguishing among these three reasons for dropping out is important because only negative dropout provides evidence of a program failure.

Negative reactions tell us that the people who enrolled in our program did not find it a satisfying experience. But dissatisfaction should not be confused with a lack of learning or other outcomes. It is quite possible for participants to be dissatisfied with some or all of the program but to have learned a great deal from it. It is also possible for participants to express high satisfaction with a program but to have learned little or nothing from it. Consequently, it cannot be assumed that positive reactions are valid evidence that learning occurred or that negative reactions are valid evidence that little or no learning occurred. Chapter Four contains an analysis of common types of negative reactions and what can be done to prevent them.

Unattained Objectives. Educational programs are planned to achieve explicit or implicit learning objectives. If objectives are not achieved, then mistakes were made somewhere in the design or delivery of the program. Although this sounds rather straightforward, determining whether there are unattained objectives is not an easy task. It is a rare program that includes a direct assessment of the degree to which objectives have been achieved. More often we see evaluation forms that ask participants to indicate the degree to which their personal objectives for attending the program have been achieved.

Understanding what the program's objectives are is the first challenge.

In some cases, program objectives are spelled out in detail at the beginning, but they often change as the program unfolds. A fair assessment of whether objectives have been achieved uses only the final, negotiated, modified objectives as the benchmark. In other cases, the program objectives are never made explicit. This causes problems when we try to evaluate the program by comparing intended learning with actual learning. Since one important purpose of educational planning is to design learning experiences with a high probability of promoting specific changes in human capability, it is impossible to determine if there are flaws in our plans or in our planning process if we do not have a clear understanding of what capabilities we are trying to change and in what way.

Another problem concerns how much change in capability is necessary or how many participants must change in the desired way before we are willing to conclude that an objective has been achieved. It is unrealistic to expect that 100 percent of the participants will achieve 100 percent of the objectives in any program. If we lack direct evidence of learning, then the best we can do is to use indirect evidence to make an informed judgment about the degree to which objectives were achieved. Indirect evidence may consist of comments from instructors or participants about what was learned and observations of how participants responded to questions posed during the program or of how they performed in role-play sessions, simulations, or problem-solving exercises.

Failure to attain objectives suggests flaws in how the expected outcomes of the program are determined or flaws in how the elements of the program are related to the objectives. Planning involves making decisions about the means required to achieve specific ends. *Good* planning involves selecting means that have a high probability of achieving the desired ends. If the desired ends (changes in human capability) are not achieved, then either the ends were inappropriate or the means were ineffective. In either case, to improve our planning skills we must understand why people's capabilities do not change in the ways we hope they will in our programs. Chapter Five focuses on what prevents people from learning what we hope they will learn and offers suggestions on what to do and what not to do to ensure that learning takes place.

Incomplete Transfer of Learning. It is one thing for people's capabilities to change as a result of their participation in an educational program, but it is another matter when they expect or are expected to apply those new capabilities in their natural environment. Participants' "natural environment" is the place where they regularly live and work, the settings where they would normally apply their new capabilities. If participants attend a program with the expectation that what they learn will be of use to them in their natural environment—and if the program is designed to promote transfer of learning to the natural environment—then a failure has occurred if transfer does not take place.

It is not always possible to follow up with participants once they have returned to the natural environment in order to determine if this transfer has occurred. Indeed, many planners and instructors in adult and continuing education would argue that their responsibility ends with designing and offering a learning experience that changes the capability of the participants as intended—that the application of learning is out of their hands, and they therefore have no obligation to ensure that learning transfer occurs. But others work in settings where transfer of learning is expected—where the reason that the participants are in the program is to help them develop capabilities that will be applied in their natural environment.

It is important to understand the reasons for incomplete transfer of learning and to separate those reasons related to the educational process and those related to other factors. Reasons related to the educational process indicate the need for changes in the planning and delivery of programs. Factors unrelated to the educational process may require changes in the participants' natural environment itself—in the reward structure, the organization of work, company policies, supervisory practices, and personnel selection, to name only a few. These are largely beyond the responsibility of the educator and must be addressed by others in the natural environment. Chapter Six is concerned with problems of transfer of learning and proposes actions that can be taken before, during, and after the program to increase the chances that learning will be applied in the natural environment.

I will make the bold claim here that the failures suggested by these five indicators are the most costly to providers of adult and continuing education programs. This is a bold claim because I have found no studies of either the extent of various types of failures or of the monetary and nonmonetary costs of failures. Work is currently under way to remedy this, but it will be some time before we have any valid estimates of either extent or costs.

Up from the Ashes

There are many lessons to be learned about successful planning from the ashes of our failures. The chapters that follow represent important contributions toward developing more refined approaches to planning—approaches that take into account not only the logic of systematic planning but also the complications that arise and the uncertainties that exist in the daily work of practitioners. Making mistakes is a natural but certainly not desirable dimension of our work. Viewing every failure as an opportunity to learn more about success is the only way to redeem what can otherwise be a lonely and dismal experience. As you read through the remaining chapters, I trust you will encounter familiar examples, useful suggestions, and new ways of thinking about your work.

References

Downs, C. M., Holt, M. E., and Taylor, M. E. "Auditing a Leisure-Program Failure." *Visions in Leisure and Business,* 1985, 4 (2-3), 40-52.

Hanson, A. L. "Anatomy of a Canceled Continuing Education Program." *American Journal of Pharmaceutical Education,* 1982, 46 (1), 23-27.

Holt, M. E., Downs, C. M., and Taylor, M. E. "Applying Systems Analysis to Program Failure in Organizations." *Innovative Higher Education,* 1986, 10 (2), 102-110.

Houle, C. O. *The Design of Education.* San Francisco: Jossey-Bass, 1972.

Lacy, C. L., and Smith, R. M. "Case Study of a Programming Success Based on a Failure." *Adult Leadership,* 1976, 25 (4), 113-115.

Lewis, T. G., and Fockler, M. E. "Help! My Training Program Bombed . . . and It Could Happen to Yours!" *Training,* 1976, 13 (6), 26-27, 30.

Martin-Lindgren, G., and Varcoe, C. M. "Postmortem Blues: Evaluating Educational Program Failures." *Nursing Management,* 1986, 17 (6), 61-63.

Smith, R. M. "A Case Study of a Programming Failure." *Adult Leadership,* 1974, 22 (8), 266, 284.

Smith, R. M. "A Case Study: No One for Puerto Rico." *Adult Leadership,* 1975, 23 (11), 322, 330.

Sork, T. J. "The Postmortem Audit: Improving Programs by Examining 'Failures.'" *Lifelong Learning: The Adult Years,* 1981, 5 (3), 6-7, 31.

Sork, T. J., Kalef, R., and Worsfold, N. E. *The Postmortem Audit: A Strategy for Improving Educational Programs.* Vancouver, British Columbia, Canada: Intentional Learning Systems, 1987.

Strother, G. B., and Klus, J. P. *Administration of Continuing Education.* Belmont, Calif.: Wadsworth, 1982.

Thomas J. Sork is associate professor of adult education at the University of British Columbia.

Practitioners perceive and explain program success and failure in a variety of ways, implying different strategies for improving the process of planning and the quality of programs.

Successful and Unsuccessful Adult Education Programs: Perceptions, Explanations, and Implications

Christine H. Lewis, Catherine C. Dunlop

> Experience is the name everyone gives to their mistakes.
> —Oscar Wilde

"Success" and "failure" are not absolute concepts that can be described in a consistent manner or accounted for with a universal explanation. They are relative terms open to subjective interpretation and application. Consequently, when used as evaluative labels for adult education programs, they inevitably conjure up an assortment of images and invoke an array of explanations depending on perspective and setting. What does a highly successful adult education program look like? What evidence indicates that a program has failed? Why are some adult education programs so successful? What factors cause other programs to be unsuccessful?

These questions formed the basis for a research project carried out recently in Vancouver, Canada (Dunlop, Lewis, and Sork, 1990). The operational objectives of the research were twofold: (1) to identify the criteria or *indicators* that practitioners use in judging an adult education program to be successful or unsuccessful and (2) to discover the causes or *factors* that practitioners associate with the success or failure of a program.

An exploration of practitioners' perceptions of success and failure is still uncharted territory in program planning research. Much of the literature consists of prescriptive program planning models that are devoid of any descriptive accounts of how planning factors actually influence the outcome of a program. The few studies that do present descriptions of how planning occurs in practice (for example, Pennington and Green, 1976) are limited by their singular focus on "successful" programs. Based on the assumption that we can learn as much, if not more, from our mistakes as from our triumphs, our research project focused not only on the "stars, winners, and smash hits" but also on the "duds, losers, and flops"—those programs that practitioners judged to be highly unsuccessful.

The literature is also deficient in its tacit acceptance of a limited view of program success. Definitions of program success are frequently linked to quantitative indicators and are biased toward the administrator's perspective (Steele, 1989). For example, Rockhill (1982) observes that "program success is defined in terms of numbers enrolled and held—a definition reinforced by funding which is dependent upon numbers enrolled" (p. 3). However, this definition of program success reflects only one of many indicators that practitioners recognize in their judgments about a program's value. Our research confirmed that practitioners consider more than enrollments when they judge a program to be highly successful and also that they are receptive to a much wider array of indicators of highly unsuccessful programs than has been previously mentioned in the literature.

After describing how the research project was carried out, the focus of this chapter turns to the main research question: What are practitioners' perceptions and explanations of successful and unsuccessful adult education programs? The chapter ends with an exploration of how the research findings can be used to increase the probability of successful programs.

Research Methodology

Sample. Since the research was exploratory in nature, the sample was designed to include different types of adult education and training programs offered within a variety of organizational settings. Interviews were conducted with thirty-two practitioners (twenty female, twelve male, having a range of two to twenty years of experience planning programs) from fourteen different agencies that provide adult education programs as either a primary or a secondary function. During the interviews, 118 programs were described by the practitioners (sixty-four "highly successful," forty-eight "highly unsuccessful," and six "mixed"). Although each practitioner was given the opportunity to discuss an equal number of highly successful and highly unsuccessful programs, many found the success stories easier to remember (hence, the uneven breakdown of the sample). Some practitioners chose to talk about "mixed" programs, which they described as containing elements of both success and failure (for example, "high enrollment" and "participants were not satisfied"). No restrictions were placed on the definition of "program." Consequently, the practitioners discussed a wide range of adult education content areas, including technical and vocational training, personal interest, public service and awareness, academic upgrading, and continuing professional development. Specific program activities mentioned by the practitioners included conferences, semester courses, evening presentations, and weekend workshops.

Table 1 shows the distribution of the programs across various agency types.

Data Collection. Semistructured interviews were used to gather data. The interviews were carried out with each practitioner at his or her place of work and lasted an average of one hour.

Two researchers were present during the interviews: One acted as the interviewer and the other took notes. The interviewer followed a format that had been developed and pretested in consultations with colleagues and in a pilot study. First, the background and the purpose of the research project were described. Then, in order to clarify the interviewer's emphasis on highly successful and highly unsuccessful programs, the practitioners were shown a continuum (using a ten-point scale) with cartoon faces and descriptive phrases at the extreme ends (see Figure 1). While many programs are moderately successful and would be positioned around the middle portion of the continuum, the practitioners were asked to focus on those programs that fell clearly within the upper and lower 20 percent. In this way, the practitioners were better able to differentiate between success and failure.

The practitioners were then asked to think about two or three specific programs that they had planned or helped to plan and that they considered to be highly successful. Discussing each program separately, the practitioners briefly described the program (its purpose, content, client group, and so on) and then responded to the following open-ended questions: (1) What were the indicators to you that this was a highly successful program? How did you know that it was a "smash hit"? (2) What factors contributed to the success of the program? What do you think accounted for its success?

Table 1. Number of Programs in the Sample, by Agency Type

Agency Types	Programs
School Board	9
University Continuing Education	23
Community College	34
Professional Association	4
Business/Industrial Firm	25
Public Education/Advocacy	8
Distance Education Agency	8
Voluntary Association	3
Government Department	4
Total	118

Figure 1. Continuum of Program Success

| 0 | 1 | 2 | 3 | 4 | 5 | 6 | 7 | 8 | 9 | 10 |

Highly Unsuccessful   Highly Successful

"dud"   "star"
"loser"   "winner"
"flop"   "smash hit"

They were then asked to think about two or three highly unsuccessful programs and to identify indicators and factors in the same manner. The final interview question asked for general comments or observations on planning successful or unsuccessful adult education programs.

Data Analysis. The actual phrases used by the practitioners in their responses to the interview questions were compiled into four comprehensive lists: (1) indicators of highly successful programs, (2) indicators of highly unsuccessful programs, (3) factors associated with highly successful programs, and (4) factors associated with highly unsuccessful programs.

Each list was examined independently by the three researchers, and similar indicators and factors were placed into categories. Through discussion, the researchers reached agreement on a common set of categories for each of the four lists.

Limitations. The exploratory nature of this study dictated how the sample was chosen, the data collected, and the responses analyzed. The sample was purposive, instead of random, in order to capture a wide variety of perspectives and settings. As such, the findings are not representative of the entire population of adult education providers, but they do provide an initial impression of practitioners' perceptions of success and failure. Second, the data were collected through semistructured interviews that gave the practitioners latitude in choosing which programs to discuss. Many practitioners chose to dwell less on the programs they classified as unsuccessful and more on the success stories. Consequently, the sample contains a higher proportion of successful programs. Analyzing failure can be very difficult and might be best approached through another data collection vehicle, such as a written survey or an intensive "postmortem audit" (Sork, 1986). Finally, an additional limitation of the research methodology was the highly interpretative nature of the data analysis. Due to the open-ended character of the interview questions, practitioners were able to provide a rich assortment of responses. Developing categories for the practitioners' responses was necessary in order to condense and clarify the findings. However, categorizing the responses was an inductive process reflecting the subjective interpretations of the research team and, as such, should be considered as only one of many possible ways to analyze and understand the interview data.

Findings

This section presents the practitioners' responses to the two main interview questions: (1) What were the indicators to you that this was a highly successful (or highly unsuccessful) program, and (2) what factors do you think contributed to the success (or failure) of this program?

Indicators. Exhibits 1 and 2 contain listings of the indicators of highly successful and highly unsuccessful programs. The indicators are arranged in descending order according to frequency of response, with the indicator mentioned most often by the practitioners at the top of the list.

It is interesting to note that many of the indicators of highly unsuccessful programs mirror (that is, are the reverse of) the indicators for highly successful programs. For example, "desired learning did not occur" in Exhibit 2 mirrors "significant participant learning occurred" in Exhibit 1.

In addition to the observation that the indicators of success and failure are often viewed by practitioners as two sides of the same coin, the findings suggest a much richer set of criteria for evaluating programs than has been previously reported in the literature. Evaluation criteria are usually linked to quantitative indicators (such as meeting financial objectives or achieving

**Exhibit 1. Indicators of Highly Successful Programs,
Ranked by Frequency of Response**

1. High demand for the program
2. Participants were satisfied
3. Increased visibility/credibility/goodwill in community
4. Significant participant learning occurred
5. High level of participant involvement/interest
6. Stakeholders were satisfied
7. Financial objectives were met
8. Produced important spin-off benefits for sponsor
9. Produced delayed/secondary benefits for participants
10. Planners/instructors were satisfied
11. High participant completion rate

**Exhibit 2. Indicators of Highly Unsuccessful Programs,
Ranked by Frequency of Response**

1. Participants were not satisfied
2. Planners/instructors were not satisfied
3. Low/disappointing enrollment
4. Financial disappointment
5. Low level of participant involvement/interest
6. Stakeholders were not satisfied
7. Programs canceled or not offered
8. Desired learning did not occur
9. High dropout rate

high enrollments) or to "happiness indexes" (scales on which participants indicate their degree of satisfaction or dissatisfaction with the program). However, this research revealed that practitioners also recognize intangible qualities of a program (for example, "increased visibility/credibility/goodwill in community") as indicators of success.

The findings also suggest that the evidence used in judging a program can come from a variety of sources. Practitioners traditionally have received feedback through a formal evaluation questionnaire handed out to the participants at the end of the program. However, as Exhibits 1 and 2 show, practitioners are also open to informal feedback, coming not only from the participants but also from instructors, colleagues, and individuals in the community.

Factors. Many of the practitioners seemed to enjoy the opportunity in the second part of the interview to sit back and speculate on why one program worked so well and another program was such a dud. Their enthusiasm for this reflective exercise might help to explain why their responses were so numerous, detailed, and insightful. Exhibits 3 and 4 contain listings of the factors associated with highly successful and highly unsuccessful programs. Again, the factors are arranged in descending order according to frequency of response, with the factor mentioned most often at the top of the list.

The question of why a program worked or did not work is complex. Therefore, it is not surprising that the factors or reasons mentioned by the practitioners were often interrelated. Many of the factors are not mutually exclusive but can be seen instead as overlapping concepts—each with a distinct core, yet sharing common elements or themes with other categories. For example, in Exhibit 3 "effective advertising/marketing" could have been included within the category "effective administration/management."

Analyzing the themes running through the lists of factors provides a useful framework for understanding how the lists change from the top to the bottom and from successful to unsuccessful programs. There are at least

Exhibit 3. Factors Associated with Highly Successful Programs, Ranked by Frequency of Response

1. Timely/relevant/innovative topic
2. Effective instructor: skills
3. Good instructional design: process
4. Good program planning/effective planner
5. Good instructional design: content
6. Effective instructor: personality
7. Practical/real-life focus
8. Caring/safe/friendly learning climate
9. Met participants' needs
10. Strong institutional support/cooperation
11. Effective administration/management
12. Effective advertising/marketing
13. Good facility/location
14. Positive relationship with client/community
15. Constant monitoring of/response to participants' reactions
16. Participants were motivated/prepared
17. Appropriate scheduling
18. Good selection/mix of participants
19. Appropriate pricing/budgeting
20. Constant monitoring of participants' learning
21. Understanding of client system and community
22. Participant involvement in planning
23. Appropriate selection of instructors
24. Customer support services

Exhibit 4. Factors Associated with Highly Unsuccessful Programs, Ranked by Frequency of Response

1. Poor instructional design: content
2. Poor program planning/ineffective planner
3. Conflicts/lack of institutional support
4. Ineffective administration/management
5. Inappropriate selection/mix of participants
6. Inadequate understanding of client group
7. Ineffective instructor: skills
8. Program did not meet a need
9. Nonsupportive/disruptive learning climate
10. Inappropriate selection/training of instructors
11. Inappropriate scheduling
12. Poor instructional design: process
13. Ineffective advertising
14. Ineffective instructor: personality
15. Inappropriate pricing/budgeting
16. Difficult relationship with client
17. Inappropriate/irrelevant/controversial topic
18. Poor facility/location

four themes or groupings found within the lists: (1) instruction, (2) administration, (3) program planning principles, and (4) interpersonal factors.

The first grouping, which revolves around instruction, consists of factors found mostly within the top portion of the list in Exhibit 3:

2. Effective instructor: skills
3. Good instructional design: process
5. Good instructional design: content
6. Effective instructor: personality
23. Appropriate selection of instructors.

Two of the factors within this grouping (numbers 3 and 5) parallel various prescriptive models in the literature (for example, Boyle, 1981) that emphasize instructional design as an essential step in the planning of successful programs. The other three factors highlight the importance of selecting an effective instructor. According to the practitioners interviewed, effective instructors can contribute to a successful program both through their skills (for example, being a good communicator or a subject matter expert) and through their personality (for example, being caring and warm or humorous and charismatic).

The second grouping clusters around administrative and managerial skills and includes the following factors:

11. Effective administration/management
12. Effective advertising/marketing
13. Good facility/location
17. Appropriate scheduling
19. Appropriate pricing/budgeting
24. Customer support services.

These administrative decisions and activities are also promoted in the literature, usually within the context of formulating an implementation plan.

The third grouping of factors relates to some of the principles of program planning found in the literature. As mentioned earlier, much of the literature consists of prescriptive models based on assumptions about adult education and the nature of the program planning process. Examples of underlying assumptions or principles of program planning found in the literature include the following: (1) Planning should be flexible (Houle, 1972); (2) programs should be based on client needs (Knowles, 1980; Boone, 1985); (3) the client system and planning context should be thoroughly analyzed (Boyle, 1981); and (4) clients should be involved in the decision-making process of program planning (Knowles, 1980; Boyle, 1981). The following factors correspond to these principles:

4. Good program planning/effective planner
9. Met participants' needs
21. Understanding of client system and community
22. Participant involvement in planning.

In contrast with the other three, the fourth and final grouping is not mentioned as much in the literature. This grouping revolves around creating and maintaining positive relationships and supportive environments. The following factors can be included in this cluster:

8. Caring/safe/friendly learning climate
10. Strong institutional support/cooperation
14. Positive relationship with client/community.

Some of the practitioners' responses that belong to this grouping contained such terms as *faith, loyalty, energy, respect, empowerment,* and *moral support.*

Before we turn to the list of factors associated with unsuccessful programs in Exhibit 4, it might be useful to consider this question: If the presence of the factors in Exhibit 3 contributes to a successful program, is it reasonable to expect that their absence will contribute to an unsuccessful program? In other words, are the lists in Exhibits 3 and 4 essentially mirror images of each other? The answer is yes. All the factors in Exhibit 4 are the reverse of factors listed in Exhibit 3. For example, "nonsupportive/disruptive learning climate" (number 9 in Exhibit 4) mirrors "caring/safe/friendly learning climate" (number 8 in Exhibit 3).

While the lists of factors associated with successful and unsuccessful programs contain many of the same ingredients, they comprise, in a sense, different recipes, since the weighting or ranking of the factors changes from one list to the other. One interesting change is the increase in frequency of response for one of the interpersonal factors when focusing on unsuccessful rather than successful programs. In Exhibit 3, "strong institutional support/cooperation" is ranked number 10, but it moves up to number 3 in Exhibit 4. This response ("conflicts/lack of institutional support") included such terms as *resistance, resentment, politics,* and *lack of trust.*

A final observation about the two lists of factors is that there are six factors on the successful programs list that were not mentioned by practitioners when discussing unsuccessful programs:

7. Practical/real-life focus
15. Constant monitoring of/response to participants' reactions
16. Participants were motivated/prepared
20. Constant monitoring of participants' learning

22. Participant involvement in planning
24. Customer support services.

This gives rise to another question that can only be answered through further research: Are there two different types of factors that contribute to highly successful programs? The first type of factor could be called "essential" and would include those factors that show up on both lists. They need to be present or carried out effectively in order to have a successful program, and if they are absent or poorly done, they will lead to an unsuccessful program. The second type of factor could be called "enhancing" and would include the six factors that only show up on the successful programs list. These factors can contribute to success, but their absence may not be associated with failure.

Implications for Practice

The findings revealed that practitioners perceive and explain program success and failure in a variety of ways. The relevance of these findings and their implications for practice now remain to be explored. This section offers some observations and practical recommendations for improving the planning process and the quality of programs.

1. *Taking the time to think about program success and failure can be valuable.* Many practitioners mentioned that they enjoyed the opportunity during the interviews to reflect on their programs. The process of analyzing program success and failure helped the practitioners to clarify implicitly held values and to determine how these assumptions were influencing their judgments about program outcomes and their expectations about program planning. By focusing on individual programs, practitioners were able to talk about success and failure in concrete terms and to recognize more readily the link between these implicitly held views and planning-related strategies and decisions.

Because program planning may involve several individuals, planners can also benefit from discussing expectations and opinions with others interested in the program (for example, with other program planners, administrators, instructors, and participants). By openly communicating with others, planners may become aware of a greater range of perceptions and explanations of program success and failure. This process may also serve to minimize the occurrence of such postmortem comments as "It's too bad we didn't talk about that before. I guess we had different expectations."

2. *The lists of indicators and factors can stimulate new ways of perceiving, planning, and evaluating programs.* The lists of indicators and factors identified in this study can be useful to practitioners who wish to improve already successful programs and to those who are grappling with a failing program.

For example, the instructional theme found within the lists of factors suggests some practical implications for planning. Because an effective instructor was considered by many of the practitioners to be an important determinant of program success, selection of the instructor could be a crucial decision for the planner. The criteria for selection mentioned by the practitioners included a dynamic and cooperative personality, use of humor, having a proven track record, and being organized, well prepared, and reliable. Practitioners shared their sad experiences of hiring a "well-known personality" who did not teach what the course advertised; of contracting with an "expert" who bored the audience to tears; of working with instructors who prepared an excellent curriculum package only to deliver it in an authoritarian manner. The lesson to be learned from these stories is that the planner should carefully consider what characteristics are important in an instructor before one is hired.

While the lists may have practical value in stimulating thinking and highlighting various perspectives, it is important to caution against using them as comprehensive, inviolate checklists for guaranteed success. Practitioners should work toward the development of individual checklists that reflect their own priorities, the unique nature of their programs, and the demands of the planning context.

3. *Integrating past experience with changing demands provides flexibility in planning.* In reflecting on previous successes and failures, the practitioners often emphasized that the planning and delivery of programs inevitably occurs within a constantly changing and often uncertain environment of shifting priorities, limited resources, and conflicting interests. Hence, the most effective approach to planning is one that integrates an awareness of the prescriptive models in the literature (which generally reflect the experience of the author), a recognition of practice wisdom gained through experience (the tried and true), and an openness to the unique demands of each program planning endeavor. This approach to planning would eliminate the problems that arise from rigidly applying a planning model to all situations or, conversely, from following an unsystematic, ad hoc approach to program planning. The dynamic interaction of the practitioner's past experience and the challenges of the current context can contribute to successful programs through a greater flexibility and responsiveness in planning.

4. *Ongoing monitoring contributes to success.* Much of program evaluation is done after the fact: A written evaluation form with ratings of satisfaction or dissatisfaction is given to participants at the end of the course. Often participants do not indicate their dissatisfaction on the evaluation form because of the perceived uselessness of the exercise (the course is over and there is no immediate benefit to them through changes in content or process) or because of a reluctance to criticize the instructor.

Many of the practitioners interviewed were aware of the limitations of this type of evaluation and therefore made it a practice to monitor the program while it was in progress. Planners who had their ear to the ground throughout the program soon became aware of a program going awry. This ongoing monitoring tends to be informal in nature, with feedback elicited from a variety of sources: coffee-break chats with participants, telephone calls to the instructors, and direct observation of the learning event in session. Practitioners' general comments during the interviews also stressed the importance of relying on one's own "gut reaction" and intuitions about a program.

While participants may be hesitant to make critical comments about a program directly to the instructor, they may be more honest with the planner, if they are two different individuals. Eliciting feedback through a third or neutral party who is neither the instructor nor the planner may also be an effective way of obtaining reliable comments from program participants.

5. *Successful program planning may require the practitioner to play a variety of roles.* The four themes found within the list of factors associated with successful programs can be related to the various roles a program planner may be called on to play. The first group of factors, concerned with instruction, suggests that the planner must be skillful in such personnel matters as the hiring and monitoring of instructors and must be knowledgeable about instructional design. The second group of factors, focusing on administrative and managerial responsibilities, implies that planners must take on the roles of financial analyst, facilities manager, public relations officer, and advertising expert. The third group, corresponding to established principles of program planning, indicates that playing the roles of community activist, demographer, and sociologist may be necessary. The fourth group, concerned with creating and maintaining positive relationships, calls for the planner to exhibit negotiation and networking skills. Thus, effective program planning is clearly more than filling seats and covering costs; it requires the planner to wear many different hats. The planner may be able to identify specific areas related to these roles when his or her professional development would benefit from continuing education courses.

The diversity of roles for the program planner may lead to potential conflict. For example, as an employee, the program planner may be directed by the organization's criteria of success, which generally focus on high enrollments and profit maximization. As an adult educator, however, the planner may be more concerned with the quality of the learning experience and with program accessibility, which might best be promoted by small class sizes and floating fee structures. If faced with this conflict, the program planner has an obligation to ensure that the educative value of the program is not jeopardized.

Conclusion

The research described in this chapter represents the first step in an attempt to ground program planning theory in actual practice (as opposed to idealized prescriptions). Discovering directly from practitioners how they think about successful and unsuccessful adult education programs and how they account for such outcomes has led to a rough sketch of perceptions and explanations. Further research will add color and detail, resulting in a more complete understanding of how planning activities are related to program outcomes.

While the sample of practitioners interviewed for this research project was small and the types of programs discussed were varied, several specific recommendations can be gleaned from the findings that may help to increase the probability of program success.

1. Make and take the time to think about what you expect from the program. Exchange your ideas with other people interested in the success of the program. Communicate, communicate, communicate!

2. Start open-ended lists of indicators and factors that you associate with successful and unsuccessful programs. Use these lists to guide your planning activities.

3. Look out for changes in the planning environment. Blend lessons learned from past experience with creative solutions for current problems. Be flexible.

4. Keep in touch with the program while it is in progress. Talk with people, visit class sessions, and listen to your own intuition. Pay special attention to possible signals of upcoming difficulties or even disasters.

5. Be prepared to wear many different hats, but don't forget the contribution you can make as an adult educator to enhancing the educative value of the program.

These recommendations can be easily applied, even under the most severe conditions of looming deadlines and constant pressure. Like a battery, they can keep a successful program running smoothly, or they can get a faltering and potentially unsuccessful program moving again.

References

Boone, E. J. *Developing Programs in Adult Education.* Englewood Cliffs, N.J.: Prentice-Hall, 1985.

Boyle, P. G. *Planning Better Programs.* New York: McGraw-Hill, 1981.

Dunlop, C. C., Lewis, C. H., and Sork, T. J. "Understanding Program Success." In B. S. Clough (ed.), *Proceedings of the 9th Annual Conference of the Canadian Association for the Study of Adult Education.* Victoria, British Columbia, Canada: University of Victoria, 1990.

Houle, C. O. *The Design of Education.* San Francisco: Jossey-Bass, 1972.

Knowles, M. S. *The Modern Practice of Adult Education: From Pedagogy to Andragogy.* (Rev. ed.) Chicago: Follett, 1980.

Pennington, F., and Green, J. "Comparative Analysis of Program Development Processes in Six Professions." *Adult Education*, 1976, 27 (1), 13–23.

Rockhill, K. "Researching Participation in Adult Education: The Potential of the Qualitative Perspective." *Adult Education*, 1982, 33 (1), 3–19.

Sork, T. J. "The Postmortem Audit: A Research Methodology for Building Inductively Derived Planning Theory." *Proceedings of the 27th Annual Adult Education Research Conference.* Syracuse, N.Y.: Syracuse University, 1986.

Steele, S. M. "The Evaluation of Adult and Continuing Education." In S. B. Merriam and P. M. Cunningham (eds.), *Handbook of Adult and Continuing Education.* San Francisco: Jossey-Bass, 1989.

Christine H. Lewis is a doctoral student in adult education at the University of British Columbia and has been involved in program planning in the areas of mental health and social services.

Catherine C. Dunlop is a doctoral student in adult education at the University of British Columbia and has a background in agricultural economics and international development.

Increased attention in program planning to issues not generally associated with educational effectiveness may help prevent cancellations because of insufficient enrollments.

Understanding Participation in Programs

Alan L. Hanson

Not all continuing education programs achieve the same level of success. Even with the most careful planning, some programs are rightfully judged as failures. The astute planner (the survivor!) will attempt to seek out the specific reasons for such failures, learn from this process, and use the knowledge gained to reduce the incidence of subsequent failures.

Continuing education programs, as viewed by both the provider and the participant, may be judged successes or failures using numerous criteria. The previous chapter suggested some of these determinants of success and failure. There are at least four general categories, presented here in summary form, in which criteria may be developed to examine and judge programs. These include (1) process (this is essentially a "happiness index" related to how well the attendees liked various program aspects, including the facility, format, arrangements, and speakers); (2) effect (the focus here is on learning outcomes, such as whether attendees acquired knowledge, attitudes, or selected skills as a result of participating in the program); (3) application (this means determining, at some point after the program is completed, to what extent the knowledge, attitudes, or skills acquired through the program have been transformed into behaviors applied in the practice setting); and (4) attendance.

This chapter focuses on the fourth category, looking in detail at the elements that influence participation in continuing education programs. The chapter is based on three assumptions: First, the major type of program under discussion is assumed to be a live program as opposed to independent learning or home study; however, this is not to suggest that home study or independent learning programs are immune from insufficient enrollments. The second assumption is that programs from which prospective participants may choose are equal in terms of educational design, content relative to the participants' work practice, and potential for success in the categories of process, effect, and application. The third assumption is that the examples provided, although based primarily on experience in planning continuing education programs in pharmacy, can be applied to programs offered to clientele in other professions and occupations.

This chapter focuses first on program planning to suggest that adherence to basic tenets of program planning does not guarantee participation. The role of budget considerations within program planning is addressed, particularly as they relate to making the decision to cancel a program. This leads to a description of the consequences of cancellation. Further discussion focuses on how to determine what other factors (not directly related to educational content or program design) may affect program participation; both retrospective and prospective case studies are presented to identify these factors. Finally, the chapter looks at noneducational factors and issues that have the potential to improve program participation.

Program Planning

The general mission of adult and continuing education providers is to offer programs that meet the educational needs of the intended audience, attract the appropriate clientele, and produce the desired changes in the participants. These changes may be cognitive, psychomotor, attitudinal, or behavioral. All of these goals must be accomplished with a positive economic outcome—that is, the programs must generate sufficient revenue to justify offering additional programs. What steps, then, should the educational provider take in order to design programs that accomplish these goals?

The Systematic Planning Model. More than twenty years ago, Boyle and Jahns (1970) suggested that an effective program "is more likely to be achieved where there has been some systematic, deliberate effort to develop a meaningful plan of action to be followed" (p. 59). They further proposed that the planning effort should include (1) a determination of the educational needs of the clientele; (2) a translation of those educational needs into objectives; (3) the design and implementation of learning experiences to achieve such objectives; and (4) an assessment of the strengths and weaknesses of the program. These four basic steps in program development, which can be traced back at least forty years in the educational literature, have provided and will continue to provide a useful framework for the development of programs.

An underlying assumption of systematic planning is that the goal— an effective program—can be achieved by following these steps. A further assumption is that the product of "good" planning will attract a sufficient number of interested persons and on that basis be judged a success. Yet if most providers of continuing education use these steps in program planning (and this assumption is open to debate!), why, judged on the basis of attendance, are some programs successful and others less successful? Perhaps the answer is that program planners, in their attempt to follow the appropriate planning steps, don't pay sufficient attention to some practical planning issues not generally identified with educational effectiveness. The budget and the program's responsiveness to the practitioners for whom it is intended are two of these issues.

Budget. The Section of Teachers of Continuing Education of the American Association of Colleges of Pharmacy (1972) includes a step in its model guidelines for the development of pharmacy continuing education programs that goes beyond the four basic planning steps just described. This added step is to identify available program resources and their limit. Thus, the planning of programs includes the consideration of the budget and the resources (personnel and dollars) required to achieve educational effectiveness. In order to achieve budgetary goals, the program must attract sufficient paying registrants to cover its development and delivery costs.

Responsiveness to Practitioners. In a discussion of the philosophy, principles, and purpose of continuing education, Hodapp (1987) refers to "six factors that make up an educationally complete continuing education program that is practitioner responsive" (p. 54). These six factors, which Hodapp attributes to Apps (1973), are quality, reasonable cost, providing personal fulfillment, offering diversity, comprehensiveness, and accessibility. In this model, the term *practitioner responsive* implies more than determining the needs of the target audience and designing the program to address those needs. It suggests that the planning process, however well conceived from the standpoint of educational effectiveness, should not lose sight of its primary focus—the practitioner in search of learning—and of the relationship that may exist between program characteristics and individual characteristics that eventually lead to program participation. For example, such program characteristics as the date it is offered, its cost, and its methods of instruction should be matched to such individual characteristics as when practitioners are most likely to attend, what they are willing and able to pay, and what instructional methods they expect and value.

Thus, there are components in program planning and design that go beyond adherence to the basic steps related to educational effectiveness, and these components will eventually contribute to the success of a program when the criterion of success is attendance. Since concerns about participation are so often tied directly to the financial aspects of planning, the following section discusses budget considerations and how they influence expectations about participation.

Budgetary Considerations

Continuing education is a business. The product to be marketed is education. There are many types of providers of continuing education; these may include academic institutions, professional associations, employers, and private entrepreneurs. There is also variation in whether the provider's continuing education enterprise is subsidized, must break even, or is required to generate a profit. In any event, there are expenses associated with the planning, marketing, and implementation of the product, and regardless of the type of provider, some revenue must be generated to meet (at least in part) or to exceed these expenses. If fees paid by program attendees are the sole or major source of revenue to offset expenses for that program, then attendance becomes crucial to its success.

Thus, beginning with the early stages of program planning, providers must pay attention to budgetary considerations. At a minimum, these considerations include a prospective and ongoing look at program costs, both fixed and variable. Fixed costs include such general, ongoing expenses as salaries and fringe benefits for program planners, as well as overhead costs (office space, utilities, supplies, equipment, and so forth). Additional fixed costs for a specific program include the costs of marketing or promotion, of the program site (room rental and audiovisuals, for example), and of speaker honoraria and expenses. Variable costs, specific to a program and tied to the number of program attendees, would include printed educational materials, meals or beverages, and evaluation.

With expenses on one side of the equation and revenue on the other, planners must consider whether there are sources of revenue that can supplement income from registration fees, which is obviously variable and linked to the number of registrants. Additional fixed sources of revenue might include subsidies or grant funds. The goal is to reconcile costs (fixed and variable) with fixed income (subsidies, grants) and variable income (registration fees). With a realistic estimate of the number of persons who would be likely to attend a given program, the provider must determine a registration fee that will generate sufficient revenue to match expenses and that will be considered reasonable by the potential attendee (in other words, a fee that is "practitioner responsive"). This target attendance figure can then serve as a criterion in determining success or failure based on participation in the program.

However, it should be pointed out that this target attendance figure, determined in advance of marketing or promotion, is not necessarily cast in concrete. Additional expenses or revenue sources may be identified at subsequent stages that may result in the modification of the target figure. But there should always be a specific target in mind so that the provider can make a decision about the program's present level of success or risk relative to attendance at any point prior to the program date.

When enrollment either exceeds or falls short of the targeted attendance figure, there can be major consequences for the budget. For example, consider a case where enrollment far exceeds predictions. Such a case might be called a success if the sole criterion is level of attendance. However, the high enrollment may severely tax the facility in which the program is held, and this may affect the program's success with regard to the first three categories of criteria: process, effect, and application. Thus, while such a scenario might be judged successful with respect to attendance and revenue, it could easily lead to failure with respect to the educational process. It may be wise to set maximum as well as minimum attendance limits and adhere to them.

If, on the other hand, enrollment is close to but slightly below the target attendance figure or if enrollment is drastically below the target figure, cancellation of the program is an option. Cancellation has an obvious impact on the budget, but there are other consequences as well. Before deciding whether to cancel a program whose enrollment is low, providers need to be aware of the possible aftermath of program cancellation.

Consequences of Program Cancellation

Program cancellation affects not only those already registered but also the facility and the program personnel (such as speakers). Consequences in each of these three areas may ultimately affect the provider.

Effect on Enrollees. Cancellation of a program may appear, at first glance, to have a limited effect on the enrollees, assuming they are provided with a full refund. However, the impact of cancellation goes beyond the registrant's initial disappointment. The registrant may have experienced the inconvenience of arranging to take time off from work or trading work days with a colleague. In some cases, there may be a financial penalty for the prospective attendee, who may have made a binding arrangement to hire a replacement for the days when the attendee planned to be absent. Arranging for "relief help" in this way is a common practice for pharmacists, for example.

Beyond these short-term problems is the lingering doubt that the potential participant may feel when the same provider markets or promotes subsequent programs. This doubt may cause prospective attendees to delay the return of registration materials or payment and to put off making appropriate arrangements for time off from work in order to see if the program will indeed be held. These delays in turn affect the program provider, who must rely on timely registrations in determining whether or not to cancel a program.

Effect on Speakers. Program cancellation can also adversely affect the scheduled speakers or program faculty. The speaker who has taken the trouble to arrange his or her schedule to participate in the program is faced with the inconvenience of any further rescheduling necessitated by the cancellation. Beyond this, many speakers are hired (formally or informally) with the unwritten assumption that an honorarium will be paid for a presentation that is to be given. In the event of program cancellation, the problem arises as to whether the speaker gets paid in full, in part, or not at all. The speaker who has devoted the time, the effort, and perhaps the expense to prepare audiovisual materials is entitled to receive some compensation. Yet compensation, from the viewpoint of the provider, is tied to revenues from registration fees that have not materialized. Another financial consequence may be penalty fees for the cancellation or change of "nonrefundable" airline tickets. Depending on how these situations are handled, the prospective speaker may not be willing to make a commitment to a future program offered by the same provider.

Effect on Facility. Cancellation also affects the facility that was supposed to serve as the program site. The facility is faced with lost revenue from sleeping rooms, meeting rooms, or meal and beverage functions due to program cancellation. Depending on the contractual arrangements, the facility may charge the provider for a portion of this lost revenue. Even if the provider is able to avoid a charge, future dealings with this facility may be affected.

Effect on Provider. Last but certainly not least, the provider is affected by the canceled program. Of most immediate concern is the financial loss that will result. Sunk costs—expenses of developing and marketing a program—must be paid for whether or not there is revenue from registration fees. An additional risk may be grant funding for the program. If the program is canceled, there may be a stipulation that any grant money received to underwrite the program must be returned to the source. Future grant funds from this or other sources may be affected by the cancellation. One of the major long-term effects of a canceled program is the credibility of the provider in the eyes of enrollees, speakers, external agencies (such as granting agencies), and the host facility. Credibility may be enhanced or hampered depending on how often the provider cancels, what type of cancellation notice is provided, and the manner in which the provider deals with these events and those involved. A provider who has planned ahead may be able to deal with the consequences in such a way as to minimize the long-term effects of cancellation.

Providers need to keep all these factors in mind when deciding whether or not to cancel a program with low enrollment. If enrollment is drastically low, cancellation may be the best alternative. However, if enrollment is below the target level but reasonably close to the target, then it may be in the best interests of the provider to proceed with the program, accepting a financial loss but maintaining credibility.

A Retrospective Look at Insufficient Enrollment

When faced with the reality of insufficient enrollment, which in turn raises the possibility of program cancellation, most providers' normal defense mechanisms take over: What's wrong with the program? Who is responsible for this mess? What did I neglect to consider? At this point, providers need to undertake a reasoned analysis of the multiple factors that lead to a person's decision to participate in a program.

Although time consuming and somewhat expensive, the most productive method for determining retrospectively people's reasons for enrolling or not enrolling is by systematically eliciting information from those for whom the program was designed. This can be accomplished through interviews (by telephone or in person), mail surveys, or a combination.

In 1982, I reported the results of a mail survey that examined the reasons for insufficient enrollment in a continuing education program for pharmacists. Planning for the original program followed the four basic steps referred to earlier in this chapter plus a fifth step focusing on resource considerations. The program was designed as a one-day seminar to be held on a Sunday in early November, and it included six hours of lecture, discussion, and small-group activities. Open-ended and structured questions in the mail survey focused primarily on noneducational issues as potential reasons for nonparticipation, but this focus did not exclude the identification of educational factors.

Survey results were examined in conjunction with an analysis of the original planning process in order to identify the factors that influenced the program's low enrollment and subsequent cancellation. Although the survey reaffirmed that Sunday was the preferred day of the week for a daylong seminar, it identified November and December as the two least desirable times of the year for a program. When asked to identify the primary reason for not registering for the program, the potential target audience listed a prior commitment; the two most common prior commitments were work and family. The second-ranked reason for not registering was a perception that the community in which the program was to be held was beyond the maximum desirable driving distance for a program.

The survey results showed that the decision to offer the program in November was a bad one for this group of professionals. The program was scheduled for November for a number of reasons. Initial planning had begun in early spring, and the planning committee had wanted to schedule the program at the earliest possible date. Due to the time needed for planning and for soliciting outside funds as a partial revenue source, to the need to avoid the summer months because of perceived conflicts with vacations as well as work schedules, and to conflicts with previously scheduled programs, November was the earliest possible month. It was also agreed to avoid later dates in November or further into the winter season due to conflicts with the holiday season and to potential problems with adverse weather, since this program was to take place in the upper Midwest.

It would be misleading to view time of year, by itself, as the only factor contributing to the program's low enrollment and subsequent cancellation.

Over half of the survey respondents had some type of conflict that prevented them from registering for the program. It should not be assumed that all would have registered had there been no conflict. Yet the types of conflicts reported (work, family, and personal) are elements that planners should be aware of but for which the planning process should not be totally faulted. Similarly, the planning process should not be blamed completely for those who, in retrospect, pointed to lack of interest in subject matter, travel distance, registration fee, and so forth as reasons for not attending. Avoiding all potential conflicts is impossible. Providers must be aware of and, to a certain extent, accept such competitive elements; further, they should be aware of and plan to meet the perceived desires of the majority unless, of course, funds are available to produce highly selective programs for a limited audience.

Although, in this example, most reasons for lack of participation were related to issues of the program's responsiveness to practitioners, something should be said about educational content and planning principles. The planning committee took what were believed to be appropriate measures in determining the subject matter for the program. The committee used a variety of information resources, including a survey of perceived needs among the target audience, past experience with programs in other locations on a similar topic, and the advice of pharmacy practitioners from the geographical area in which the program was to be held. Certainly, prudent planners should utilize various methods, alone or in combination, to select potential subject matter, including interest surveys, self-perceived need surveys, advanced techniques that determine actual needs or deficiencies, advice from planning committees, and personal beliefs. However, even though multiple methods are used, the provider may still pick a topic that may not generate the desired response if he or she misreads surveys that identify needs or interests. Needs are not the same as interests, and an expression of priorities with respect to either one does not, in itself, ensure participation.

A Prospective Analysis of Barriers to and Facilitators of Participation

Hanson and DeMuth (1990) surveyed a 0.5 percent random sample of licensed pharmacists in the United States to determine factors that facilitate or impede their participation in professional continuing education. The questionnaire included sixteen potential barriers to participation and twelve potential facilitators. Respondents utilized a seven-point Likert scale to identify the extent (ranging from "always" to "never") to which each of these factors served as facilitators of or barriers to their participation in continuing professional education in the previous twelve-month period. An examination of this entire data set is beyond the scope of this chapter.

However, a brief look at the top-ranked barriers and facilitators should be of interest. The top-ranked barrier to participation consisted of job constraints, such as lack of relief help or lack of time off. The next three barriers, listed in decreasing order of importance, included scheduling (location, distance, time) of group learning activities, family constraints (spouse, children, personal), and lack of relevance of learning opportunities known to be available. With respect to these top four barriers, only two demographic variables showed any significant relationships. To no one's surprise, pharmacists employed on a full-time basis perceived job constraints as a greater barrier to participation in continuing education than those employed part time. Further, family constraints and scheduling of programs were perceived as greater barriers to participation by those pharmacists in the middle-age categories (thirties first, followed by forties), which are likely to correspond to those times in life in which many people have greater family responsibilities.

The greatest facilitator of participation in continuing professional education was a personal desire to learn (intellectual curiosity). Additional top-ranked facilitators, listed in decreasing order of importance, include requirement for maintenance of professional licensure; enjoyment or relaxation provided by learning as a change of pace from the routine; and opportunity to meet, interact, and exchange ideas with others.

This ranking or prioritizing of barriers and facilitators reveals pharmacists' perceptions of the impact of the listed factors on their participation in programs. Although these perceptions give us some general ideas about barriers that might be decreased or facilitators that might be enhanced in order to promote increased participation, the difficulty in drawing widespread conclusions is that the sixteen barriers and twelve facilitators do not necessarily represent the universe of potential barriers and facilitators. The other unknown factor is how facilitators and barriers interact. As a person determines whether or not to attend a specific program, multiple facilitators and barriers may be interacting at one time. The relative weight or impact of one facilitator versus one barrier is not clear. Research in deterrents to participation (Scanlan and Darkenwald, 1984; Valentine and Darkenwald, 1990) is contributing to an improved understanding of the complexity of a person's decision to participate in an educational program.

Improving the Potential for Participation

The retrospective and prospective case studies just described, although they were conducted nearly a decade apart and used different target audiences (one restricted to a segment of one state while the other was national in scope), yielded remarkably similar results. In both cases, conflicts with work, family, or personal interests appeared to have the potential for a major negative impact on participation in continuing professional education. Predominant reasons for nonparticipation centered on different aspects of the program's accessibility. These findings appear to lend credence to the position stated earlier in this chapter: Adherence in program planning to educational principles alone does not ensure satisfactory levels of participation. Rather, additional attention must be paid to characteristics of the program that make it practitioner responsive. What can providers do to make their programs, designed for educational effectiveness, more responsive to the potential participants? The paragraphs that follow address four general areas that affect a program's responsiveness: (1) determination of the target audience; (2) promotion and marketing; (3) competition in programming; and (4) logistics of program design.

Target Audience. Providers may wish to devote increased attention to determining who the target audience is for the programs they are planning. This sounds simple, but in reality it may not be. If the provider is developing a program for social workers, the target audience is usually presumed to be any and all social workers; if the provider is developing programs for pharmacists, the target audience is usually presumed to be any and all pharmacists. But determining the target audience is generally not this straightforward. For example, in the profession of pharmacy, there are multiple specialty areas for which educational programming might be designed, including managerial, therapeutic, and communication topics, to name a few. If a program in one of these specific areas is designed to appeal to the general population of pharmacists, it will probably be only marginally interesting to the specialists themselves. In other words, providers should not dilute their programs in an attempt to make them of general interest to all people within their target group; instead, they should aim programs at a more selectively defined audience.

Marketing and Promotion. Segmenting a market and promoting a program to a selective target audience require a certain amount of expertise. That expertise can be gained through course work, degree programs, and experience. In other words, focusing more closely on a selective target audience implies the need to pay increased attention to promotion and marketing. .

Promotional material should contain a complete and accurate description of the program, ranging from program title to goals, objectives, and who would benefit most from attending the program. What appears to be obvious to providers in terms of program description may not be quite so obvious to the target population. For example, I marketed a program for the general population of pharmacists focusing on legitimate and illegitimate drug use by athletes. Although the program dealt primarily with pharmacological agents, the program was titled "Sports Medicine." Program attendance was lower than anticipated. Evaluations suggested that the program's title should have more accurately reflected the content. Even though the promotional brochure described the content under program objectives, the actual participants guessed that those who did not attend may not have read beyond the program title. After all, professionals are bombarded with a plethora of promotional information. Such materials must allow the professional to make an informed decision about whether a program will meet his or her needs. In addition, providers might consider advertising a telephone number through which interested members of the target group can get assistance in selecting the most suitable programs.

Competition. The program provider who has made the effort to focus on the appropriate audience and has promoted the program appropriately should not fail to scan the competitive marketplace to see what other programs are being offered that may draw attendance away from his or her program. All other efforts may be for nought if a competitor is offering a program to the same clientele close to or on the identical dates. Such competition can have an adverse effect on participation levels regardless of the educational quality of either program. One option is to network with other known providers to determine what additional programming is taking place; this may lead to a cooperative arrangement, beneficial to a number of parties, in which competitors share information regarding program topics and dates and make sincere attempts to avoid head-to-head competition. This arrangement may not work for everyone, but it has worked for me.

Providers should also be aware of internal competition—that is, programs offered by the same provider organization that may compete with each other for a limited audience. If the addition of one other program to a provider's mix of offerings simply redistributes the attendees from one program to the next without increasing the total number of attendees for all programs, the provider must ask what has been gained—other than increased administrative work.

Program Logistics. Although this area may fall within the usual realm of program design, it deserves attention by itself. Program logistics include decisions about, among other things, location (city or specific facility), time of year, day of week, and overall length of program. An important goal in making these decisions is to be responsive to the practitioner by enhancing accessibility to the program. In choosing the city in which to conduct the program, the provider must consider where the *demographic* center, rather than the geographic center, of the target audience is.

Time of year and day of week have been addressed as issues in the retrospective case study; each provider should be aware of these factors as they pertain to a specific target population. It is of paramount importance to avoid religious and other holidays as well as days immediately preceding or following these holidays, since many people use these periods for family or leisure activities. The issue of holidays becomes more complicated for those providers who schedule international meetings. Knowledge of holidays and important occasions in the country in which the meeting will be held and in those countries where the potential participants reside is critical.

The final factor to be addressed within the area of logistics is the length of the program. Obviously, a program should be of sufficient duration to accomplish the educational objectives. However, the overall length of the program does affect accessibility. Time spent at a program is time spent away from work, from home, and from family. These have all been identified as significant barriers to participation. In addition, both the length of the program and the distance from the attendee's residence to the program location will affect such attendee expenses as meals, lodging, and work replacements. Providers must be sensitive to all of these issues as they design programs for optimum attendance.

Conclusion

Perhaps it is next to impossible to plan and implement a program that will be 100 percent responsive to all its potential clientele. However, this does not excuse the program provider from considering the various factors contributing to client responsiveness and from attempting to address as many of these as possible in the final program design. As I mentioned in the discussion of program planning, adherence to the basic design steps related to educational content cannot guarantee that sufficient attendance will be achieved. Neither will efforts to address additional issues of client responsiveness (such as accessibility) ensure sufficient attendance. On the other hand, to ignore such factors is as close as a continuing education provider can get to a guarantee of program failure.

References

Apps, J. W. "Toward a Working Philosophy of Adult Education." *Publications in Continuing Education (Occasional Papers)*, no. 36. Syracuse, N.Y.: Syracuse University, 1973.

Boyle, P. G., and Jahns, I. R. "Program Development and Evaluation." In R. M. Smith, G. F. Aker, and J. R. Kidd (eds.), *Handbook of Adult Education.* New York: Macmillan, 1970.

Hanson, A. L. "Anatomy of a Canceled Continuing Education Program." *American Journal of Pharmaceutical Education,* 1982, 46 (1), 23–27.

Hanson, A. L., and DeMuth, J. E. "Facilitators and Barriers to Pharmacists' Participation in Lifelong Learning." Paper presented at the 1st International Conference on Lifelong Learning in Pharmaceutical Sciences and Services, Hillerod, Denmark, May 10, 1990.

Hodapp, W. J. "Philosophy, Principles, and Purpose." In J. R. Arndt and S. J. Coons (eds.), *Continuing Education in Pharmacy.* Alexandria, Va.: American Association of Colleges of Pharmacy, 1987.

Scanlan, C., and Darkenwald, G. G. "Identifying Deterrents to Participation in Continuing Education." *Adult Education Quarterly,* 1984, 34, 155–166.

Section of Teachers of Continuing Education of the American Association of Colleges of Pharmacy. "Guidelines for Continuing Pharmaceutical Education." *American Journal of Pharmaceutical Education*, 1972, *36*, 642-644.

Valentine, T., and Darkenwald, G. G. "Deterrents to Participation in Adult Education: Profiles of Potential Learners." *Adult Education Quarterly*, 1990, *41*, 29-42.

Alan L. Hanson is professor of pharmacy in the School of Pharmacy, University of Wisconsin–Madison, and administers the continuing education programs for practicing pharmacists and personnel employed at all levels of the pharmaceutical industry.

Understanding the most common mistakes that lead to negative reactions to programs can help us plan more satisfying learning experiences.

How to Avoid Negative Reactions to Programs

Robert G. Simerly

Picture this scenario. You have just conducted a two-day executive development program entitled "Dealing with Upset Citizens and the Public." Because of your effective marketing efforts, the program attracted over 150 people, which was 100 more than necessary to break even financially. The facilities were excellent, and the food was good. However, after the program was over, several participants informed you that it wasn't worth the money. In fact, two people called the day after the program and demanded a refund. An analysis of the evaluations revealed that most participants rated the program as average to poor, with few people indicating an overall reaction of average or above. You and your staff had worked hard at making the program a success. What went wrong? Why did so many participants have a less-than-positive reaction?

Similar scenarios are part of the experience of almost all continuing education program planners at some time in their professional lives. How can program planners learn from their failures? How can they minimize negative reactions? How can they develop a set of positive guidelines that will maximize program success? How can they avoid making the most common mistakes in this area?

This chapter is devoted to identifying and analyzing ten of the most common negative reactions to programs. Analyzing the reasons for those reactions and implementing guidelines designed to guard against them can help produce excellent programming with satisfied clients. These are practical suggestions that have worked in a wide variety of continuing education settings in both the profit and nonprofit sectors. They apply equally to large and small programs.

NEW DIRECTIONS FOR ADULT AND CONTINUING EDUCATION, no. 49, Spring 1991 © Jossey-Bass Inc., Publishers

The Ten Most Common Negative Reactions

1. *The program did not meet my expectations.* This is a frequently heard complaint from some attendees. In the absence of clearly stated program goals, attendees will arrive with a wide variety of expectations (Knox, 1986; Brookfield, 1986, 1987; Nadler and Nadler, 1987; Simerly and Associates, 1989). This often puts presenters as well as program planners in a no-win situation.

For example, for a workshop entitled "Dealing with Upset Citizens and the Public," attendees may have any of the following expectations when they arrive, if the program's goals have not been clearly stated: Some will expect to learn new skills in dealing with upset citizens. Others will expect to find ways to prevent citizens from being upset in the first place. Others may expect to learn new ways to overcome all criticism through more effective public relations campaigns. Others may want to find out about the latest research on working effectively with a dissatisfied public. And still others may expect to learn one all-encompassing technique for dealing with upset citizens. Thus, program planners must develop clearly stated program goals, include these in all publicity, reinforce them when introducing each program session, and create evaluations that determine how effectively the goals were met. Here are some possible goals to include in the direct-mail brochure for "Dealing with Upset Citizens and the Public":

- To present ten effective ways for dealing with upset citizens and the public
- To practice skill building in simulated situations in order to illustrate effective ways for dealing with upset citizens
- To understand better what upsets citizens and to show how this knowledge is an important first step in dealing effectively with people and their concerns
- To examine twelve techniques you can implement in your office tomorrow in order to decrease the likelihood that you will have upset citizens in the first place
- To develop an action plan for dealing with upset citizens.

In addition, program planners can improve the chances of attracting participants with similar interests by specifying as clearly as possible exactly who should attend the program. For example, the brochure for "Dealing with Upset Citizens and the Public" might include the following information:

Who Should Attend?

Employees at all levels of public and private organizations who have contact with citizens and the public will benefit from this workshop. Whether you handle restaurant complaints about cold food or county complaints about increased land valuations, there are techniques that can help you deal effectively with the public.

The important thing is that direct-mail advertising and other forms of communication, such as registration acknowledgment letters, clearly state the goals of the program, accurately describe the content, and specify the types of people who should attend. When this is done, the planner has minimized the possibility that people will arrive with a wide variety of conflicting expectations.

2. *I did not like the method of presentation.* Some people prefer lecture presentations; others like small, informal work groups where there is an opportunity for much discussion and interaction. Others like large-group discussion so that everyone at the program hears the same information. Some people like the use of case studies while still others like hands-on simulations.

Given these different learning styles, program planners must help participants arrive at the program with a similar set of expectations regarding the method of instruction that will be used. Often this is not an easy task. However, it is important to clarify this issue as much as possible in all advertising for the program. For example, the following copy would be appropriate to include in the direct-mail brochure for "Dealing with Upset Citizens and the Public":

Workshop Format
    Since the goals of the program are to help participants become more skilled at dealing with upset citizens and the public, the two-day program will use a workshop format. Case studies will be cited. Small-group discussions will be held. Short lectures will help you understand how to be more effective in dealing with the public. Simulations will be conducted in which you will have the opportunity to role play the handling of a difficult situation with an upset citizen. Thus, the wide variety of program presentation methods is designed to help you become more effective back home on the job.

This description communicates that there will be reasonably high participant involvement throughout the program, and people can make their decisions about whether to attend based on this information. This helps increase participant satisfaction with the entire program.

3. *There was not enough time to socialize and swap information with colleagues.* People attend programs for a wide variety of reasons. Some come because they are genuinely interested in the content. Others are sent by their bosses in the hope that the program will provide remedial work or correct deficiencies in their job performance. Some attend because their friends are

coming and they do not wish to be left out. Others attend because they will be viewed negatively by their home organizations if they do not. Some attend in order to get away from the office for a little rest and relaxation. And still others attend expecting to gain many new skills that will dramatically change their lives.

How can program planners create programs in which the widely varying motivations of many participants can be addressed? One thing we know from research on attendee motivation is that the opportunity to socialize is an important attraction for most attendees. In fact, I have conducted many marketing research focus groups with attendees. The findings are consistent across all content areas in the conference business. One of the main reasons people attend programs is to see their friends, make new professional friends, and swap ideas about how to implement new concepts back home. In fact, often participants in these focus groups admit that the actual program content is of secondary importance when compared to the social rewards they gain from attending.

In view of these findings, planners need to build into the schedule adequate formal and informal time for socializing. Some ways to do this are to plan half-hour rather than ten-minute refreshment breaks in the morning and afternoon; plan luncheons that last an hour and a half instead of an hour; and number people's name tags and arrange meal functions so people with the same number sit at the same table. This is an easy way to help strangers develop new friendships. Planners should structure workshop sessions so that people can meet in small groups to discuss ideas for implementing new concepts in their home situations. Giving attention during the planning process to the socialization needs of participants is critical to overall program success.

4. *The program ran behind schedule, which showed a lack of planning.* It is important that program planners develop a realistic schedule, publish program timetables as appropriate, and then stick to the announced schedule. For example, at a small program where all participants are in the same room at the same time, it is often inappropriate to list times other than the beginning and ending times for the entire program. This provides considerable flexibility for the group leader to adjust content according to the discussion that may emerge. With larger programs involving concurrent sessions, it is important to work with presenters ahead of time to ensure that their presentations begin and end on time. It is also important to allow enough time for breaks and meals. Frequently, in an effort to pack as much content into a program as possible, planners underestimate the amount of time necessary for breaks, meals, and other social activities. For example, it is almost impossible to provide a large luncheon for several hundred people in less than an hour and a half. If planners allow only an hour in the schedule, people probably will not finish on time. This, in turn, will throw off any published time-

table. Nothing communicates a sense of ineffective planning faster than announcing specific times for particular program segments, including meals and breaks, and then not adhering to the announced times.

5. *The program was not practical enough to help me in my home situation.* If the purpose of a program is to provide practical information to help people in their jobs back home, there are a number of things program planners can do to ensure this happens (Simerly, 1990). First, they can emphasize to all program presenters that presentations must be applicable to the participants' natural environment. An easy way to accomplish this is to ask presenters to submit an outline describing their central idea, the exact program content, and five or ten practical things they will emphasize. Asking presenters to spell these items out in writing before the program will ensure that they are aware of the importance of gearing their presentations to practical information. Second, you can ask presenters to include as part of the summary to their presentation specific practical suggestions to implement back home. For example, after a morning presentation on techniques for dealing with upset citizens, a program presenter might conclude in the following manner:

> This morning's session has dealt with five practical suggestions for you to consider implementing in your situation back home:
>
> 1. How to answer the person who has raised his or her voice when talking to you—You will recall that during the role-playing situation we identified two examples of effective responses. Let's briefly review these. . . .
>
> 2. How to say no when no other answer is appropriate—Again, in the role-playing situation we saw how important it was to communicate to upset citizens the fact that you genuinely care about them even though you must say no.
>
> 3. How to keep your cool when a citizen is being abusive—Who can summarize for us the three helpful hints we examined for this situation? [Wait for audience response.]
>
> 4. How to step into the other person's shoes and understand the problem from his or her point of view—From the list we created, what are five of the most effective ways for doing this? [Wait for audience response.]
>
> 5. How to listen effectively—In the workshop we illustrated the importance of clearly distinguishing among active, passive, and responsive listening. Let's just review these examples again for reinforcement.

While this level of detail is often not appropriate in summaries for shorter presentations, it is appropriate for longer, hands-on workshops. Program planners must not assume that presenters will offer this kind of summary reinforcement; instead, they must work with presenters to ensure that effective summaries are given in order to help achieve overall program goals.

6. *I did not get good preprogram service.* Service-oriented organizations pay a great deal of attention to how clients are handled during any and all contacts (Albrecht and Zemke, 1985; Desatnick, 1987; Freedman, 1987; Zemke and Schaaf, 1988, 1989). For example, when people send in their registration, they expect it to be acknowledged promptly—usually within twenty-four to forty-eight hours. Waiting longer communicates a lack of concern with client service on the part of the sponsoring organization. Acknowledgments should be prompt and should thank the person for registering. Information about beginning program hours as well as location should be included in the acknowledgment.

Prospective attendees may call for additional information. How they are handled on the phone often affects whether they actually register or not. An appropriate response when answering all phone calls is "Hello, this is Bob Simerly in the Division of Continuing Studies. How may I help you?" In other words, program planners should analyze all client contact from a total systems point of view to ensure that everyone gets excellent preprogram service.

7. *I could not figure out how to implement new ideas from the program in my home situation.* This is a frequent complaint heard in relation to programs where specific skill building is a goal. Although the new skills and ideas sound fine in the workshop setting, participants sometimes have difficulty identifying how they can use these skills and concepts back home.

Personal change, if it is to be effective, needs to be supported by the overall culture of the participants' home organizations. However, it is possible to give participants time during the program to think about the issue of applying what they have learned and to get ideas on how they might proceed. One of the best ways to do this is to allow time toward the end of the program for participants to develop an action plan. Figure 1 shows what such an action plan might look like.

The action plan form should be given to participants at the beginning of the program. Encourage them during the course of presentations to write down ideas they would like to consider implementing back home. Then save time at the end of the program to have them fill out the remainder of the form: identifying the appropriate person to implement the idea, defining what resources will be needed, and considering constraints that may hinder implementation as well as positive things that can help promote the specific change. Save the last column for additional remarks.

After participants have identified several issues on their action plan, form small groups where people can share their ideas and possible implementation strategies and can get feedback on how best to proceed. Program planners who use action implementation plans consistently report that this can be one of the most powerful parts of the program. It is essential, however,

Figure 1. Action Plan for Implementing Ideas Back Home

Idea	Person to Implement	Resources Needed	Constraints to Hinder Implementation	Positive Things to Promote Change	Additional Remarks

that participants be given enough time to think through ideas thoroughly, present them in small-group situations, and get advice from the group. Many planners find that a half hour at the end of a day's program is required in order for participants to work through an implementation plan effectively.

Action plans are a way to empower people, giving them the sense that they have the power to suggest changes in their organizations. Achieving this sense of personal empowerment, in turn, helps to create an organizational culture that encourages individual initiative and effective problem solving (Deal and Kennedy, 1982; Block, 1987; Vaill, 1989; Cohen and Bradford, 1990).

8. *The program presentations did not take into account the cultural diversity of the audience.* Program presenters need to be aware of the major components of an overall concern for cultural diversity. Cultural diversity includes issues of gender, race, ethnicity, age, and cultural background. This means that program presentations and handouts must avoid sexist language and references to racial or ethnic stereotypes and must actively communicate that cultural diversity is valued.

To promote this important idea of valuing cultural diversity, the National University Continuing Education Association has adopted the following statement:

Cultural Diversity Statement of Intent
The National University Continuing Education Association affirms its commitment to recognize and value the ethnic and racial richness of our

nation and to encourage and foster mutual respect and understanding among all women and men in its membership and on the campuses of member institutions. We recognize that true excellence in an organization results from identifying and enlisting the participation of women and men who represent the rich diversity of our nation's heritage.

As an association, NUCEA values and encourages the participation of all people who endorse the principles and ideals of continuing education, including individuals from diverse backgrounds, and has taken official action to promote the expanded involvement of women and racial and ethnic group members. We acknowledge an unfortunate history in our country of the use of derogatory, stereotypical, and other nonproductive characterizations of racial and ethnic group members and women, and we resolve to eliminate such portrayals and language from all NUCEA communications and forums.

NUCEA affirms the policy that anyone speaking as an NUCEA representative, or as a guest speaker in an NUCEA forum, will acknowledge the diversity of our membership and our commitment to honor and treat with dignity all people, whether or not they are represented, and by using language that is nonsexist and respectful of all cultures.

Further, we believe that as a professional organization, we can and should play an integral role in promoting a greater appreciation of and healthier regard for the growing diversity of our campus communities. NUCEA, through its involvement with specific campus programs and activities, as well as through the actions of its members and official representatives, is dedicated to demonstrating to the higher education community its commitment to equity for all persons regardless of race, ethnicity, or gender.

> Adopted by the NUCEA Board of Directors,
> April 1990

Program planners should create a similar policy statement, adapted to the individual needs of their organization, and should give it to all program presenters. This serves as an important signal that your organization values cultural diversity, and it emphasizes that all presenters must be sensitive to these issues during their presentations or in any handouts or visuals they may use.

9. *I wasted my time because I already knew most of the program content.* The easiest way to avoid attracting these participants is to provide a detailed outline of the program content in all advertising. For example, the advertising for the two-day workshop on dealing with upset citizens and the public might use the following content outline in the direct-mail brochure:

1. Determining citizen problems and concerns
   a. Asking the right questions

    b. Listening effectively
    c. Using positive nonverbal communication
    d. Identifying problems rather than symptoms
    e. Understanding the citizen's point of view
    f. Helping the public find satisfaction.
2. Handling angry and demanding citizens
    a. Defusing potentially explosive situations
    b. Confronting an angry citizen
    c. Disagreeing without becoming argumentative
    d. Saying no and meaning it
    e. Using powerful words to get your point across
    f. Keeping your cool when a citizen is being abusive
    g. Turning an angry citizen into a responsive citizen.
3. Presenting a positive image to the public
    a. Giving personalized service
    b. Conveying respect
    c. Using courtesy and tact
    d. Establishing comfort, rapport, and trust
    e. Maintaining a positive attitude in dealing with the public.

If a reader already knows the content described, he or she can elect not to attend. However, if potential participants find a number of items about which they would like to learn more, they may want to register for the program. Such clarity in the marketing materials helps prevent the presence of bored attendees in the audience and decreases the likelihood that providers will hear this complaint.

10. *As a presenter, I was unhappy with the program.* There are three basic types of negative reactions that typically come from program presenters. First, presenters sometimes complain they were given incomplete information about the audience, purpose of the program, goals of their session, or expectations for outcomes. Second, between the time they accept an invitation to be part of a program and the time when it actually occurs, presenters sometimes complain that they received little or no guidance from the program planners regarding expectations for their segment of the program. Third, they sometimes note that an "unfair" evaluation was designed for their sessions—an evaluation that did not relate to their overall goals. Therefore, they reject any evaluation of their contributions as invalid. Here are some positive steps to take that will help avoid these negative reactions.

First, it is important to give program presenters a comprehensive description of the composition of the audience, the expectations of the audience, the goals of the program, the goals of the presenter's session (which program planners should work out collaboratively with each presenter), and other pertinent information that will assist them in planning the best possible presentation. Do not rely only on oral communication for this. While arrangements may be worked out orally initially, they should be followed up with a detailed, written summary of these issues. In writing up this information, planners should keep in mind that between the time a presenter confirms and the time the presentation takes place, many other demands on a presenter's time will occur. Therefore, presenters need written documentation to which they can refer while they plan their program.

Second, in order to ensure that the presenters prepare adequately, planners must communicate with them periodically between the time they are confirmed and the actual time of their presentation. Send out notes of confirmation. Call them. Send copies of all advertising. Write down the goals of the overall program. Ask them to send you the specific goals for their part of the program. Ask for a detailed outline of the content they will cover. Shortly before the beginning of the program, reconfirm with them the content they will be covering.

Third, evaluations should be clearly related to the established goals for each program presenter's session (Simerly, 1990). Do not fall into the trap of pulling out a generic evaluation form from the bottom drawer and assuming that it will be appropriate for all presenters. For example, a frequent mistake is to ask the following question on an evaluation form:

How well did this presentation meet your expectations?
_____ Very well
_____ Above average
_____ Average
_____ Below average
_____ Poor

The danger in asking this question is that participants often arrive with a wide variety of expectations that are sometimes impossible to fulfill. Evaluation, in order to be as effective and helpful as possible, should always be related to clearly established goals. For example, a better way to seek reactions is to state the major goal for a presentation and then ask participants to evaluate the presenter in relation to this goal:

The goal for this workshop session was to present five effective ways to deal with upset citizens. How well do you feel this session met this goal?
_____ Very well
_____ Above average
_____ Average
_____ Below average
_____ Poor

Taking time to develop evaluations individualized to the goal of each program or each segment of the program will go a long way toward ensuring that program presenters are satisfied with the validity of evaluation results.

Work out with presenters in advance exactly what the goals will be for their presentations; then list these goals on the evaluation form and ask the participants to evaluate all presentations in relation to these goals. This helps participants focus on the fact that there were specific goals and that evaluation is not just a popularity contest to see who was most effective in pleasing the crowd. Working actively with presenters during program planning can virtually eliminate dissatisfaction in this area of evaluation (Simerly, 1990).

Summary

This chapter has examined ten major negative reactions to programs. Guidelines have been presented to help program planners engage in the type of planning that will avoid these negative reactions. People react negatively for specific reasons. Understanding these reasons and addressing these dynamics through effective planning is an important leadership skill for all program planners.

References

Albrecht, K., and Zemke, R. *Service America! Doing Business in the New Economy.* Homewood, Ill.: Dow Jones–Irwin, 1985.

Block, P. *The Empowered Manager: Positive Political Skills at Work.* San Francisco: Jossey-Bass, 1987.

Brookfield, S. D. *Understanding and Facilitating Adult Learning: A Comprehensive Analysis of Principles and Effective Practices.* San Francisco: Jossey-Bass, 1986.

Brookfield, S. D. *Developing Critical Thinkers: Challenging Adults to Explore Alternative Ways of Thinking and Acting.* San Francisco: Jossey-Bass, 1987.

Cohen, A. R., and Bradford, D. L. *Influence Without Authority.* New York: Wiley, 1990.

Deal, T. E., and Kennedy, A. A. *Corporate Cultures: The Rites and Rituals of Corporate Life.* Reading, Mass.: Addison-Wesley, 1982.

Desatnick, R. L. *Managing to Keep the Customer: How to Achieve and Maintain Superior Customer Service Throughout the Organization.* San Francisco: Jossey-Bass, 1987.

Freedman, L. *Quality in Continuing Education: Principles, Practices, and Standards for Colleges and Universities.* San Francisco: Jossey-Bass, 1987.

Knox, A. B. *Helping Adults Learn: A Guide to Planning, Implementing, and Conducting Programs.* San Francisco: Jossey-Bass, 1986.

Nadler, L., and Nadler, Z. *The Comprehensive Guide to Successful Conferences and Meetings: Detailed Instructions and Step-by-Step Checklists.* San Francisco: Jossey-Bass, 1987.

Simerly, R. G. *Planning and Marketing Conferences and Workshops: Tips, Tools, and Techniques.* San Francisco: Jossey-Bass, 1990.

Simerly, R. G., and Associates. *Handbook of Marketing for Continuing Education.* San Francisco: Jossey-Bass, 1989.

Vaill, P. B. *Managing as a Performing Art: New Ideas for a World of Chaotic Change.* San Francisco: Jossey-Bass, 1989.

Zemke, R., and Schaaf, D. "The Service Edge." (Audio tape.) Minneapolis, Minn.: Lakewood Publishing, 1988.

Zemke, R., and Schaaf, D. *The Service Edge: 101 Companies That Profit from Customer Care.* New York: New American Library, 1989.

Robert G. Simerly is dean of the Division of Continuing Studies and professor of adult education at the University of Nebraska, Lincoln.

Educators must attend to issues large and small that can get in the
way of the learning process.

Why They Didn't Learn What We
Wanted Them to Learn

P. Bailey Allard

It happened again last week. I arrived in Calgary, but my materials did not.
I know better. I thought I had planned better. I have been leading training
programs for over twelve years. I have taught on every continent in the free
world except Antarctica. Still, it happened. As I was trudging all over town
frantically trying to assemble a last-minute substitute for participant materials, I kept muttering to the beat of my feet, "Mistakes made, lessons
learned. Mistakes made, lessons learned."

This chapter is about errors in planning that affect participants' learning. Having materials stuck in customs was a simple administrative glitch,
but a glitch that dramatically impacted the trainer, the quality of the training experience, and, ultimately, the quality of learning.

That experience set the stage for reviewing the components, large and
small, that get in the way of effective continuing education. I classified this
one as carelessness. There are other categories: confusion, lack of commitment, lack of clarity and courage, and lack of cultural sensitivity. Failure to
pay attention to these planning issues may result in lack of credibility for
the program, the leader, or the process itself. When participants do not
perceive the process as credible, they "shut down," or rather they fail to
"open up," to become receptive to learning.

The question for practitioners, then, is how to establish and maintain
receptivity to the program and the process. No theory will be espoused
here. All the comments spring from the personal experiences of corporate
curriculum developers and trainers.

NEW DIRECTIONS FOR ADULT AND CONTINUING EDUCATION, no. 49, Spring 1991 © Jossey-Bass Inc., Publishers

Carelessness

When the participants arrived for the assertiveness program, there was no course leader to greet them. They waited patiently, fifteen minutes, thirty minutes, one hour. Still no course leader. At 9:30 A.M., someone in the class made a telephone call. An hour late? It was, after all, an assertiveness training class. The problem? An instructor scheduling oversight. An unprepared trainer was hastily rushed to the classroom to begin the class two hours late. All the planning, the setting of objectives, and the design methodology fell apart because of careless administration. Neither the class nor the trainer was able to recover from such a poor beginning.

Participants begin to assess a program before they even enter the room. Brochures, confirmation letters, prework assignments, even telephone conversations are all used by participants to decide what the program is really about, whether it will be worth their time, what they can honestly expect to learn from the program, and how much the resource people know about the subject.

Data General Corporation has a corporate training center in the rural community of Woodstock, Connecticut. The training organization spent months developing a comprehensive training program for newly hired employees, and sales representatives from many countries were expected to attend. When two "new hires" from Europe arrived at Boston airport after a long and wearisome flight, they asked the car rental agent for directions to Woodstock. Everyone has heard of Woodstock, right? A classic case of mistaken assumptions on everyone's part sent those two off in the wrong direction. The rental agent knew the employees would not be driving to Woodstock, New York (location of the famous sixties rock festival). Instead, they were given directions to Woodstock, Vermont. It took many hours of driving and several inquiries before these first-time visitors realized they had ended up three states away from their destination. The confirmation letter had indicated, but had not emphasized, Woodstock, *Connecticut.* Two travel-weary internationals arrived six hours late for the beginning of a two-week orientation program. How much credibility did this program have in their bleary eyes?

A scene from the movie *The Electric Horseman* summarizes this issue well. In that film, a beautiful but aging horse that served as a corporate symbol for the Acme Corporation was stolen. Acme's chief executive officer was emphatic that they must get the horse back at all costs. "Why?" asked his aides. "It's just a horse. What's the big deal?" But the CEO understood what his aides took lightly. "It's a very big deal. In the minds of the public, if we mismanage the horse, we mismanage the corporation."

The same thing goes for training programs. Sloppy room setup, poorly organized participant materials, missing or out-of-date handouts that don't match the instructor's slides, and equipment that does not work or continues to break down are all examples of ways in which classes bomb due to carelessness, no matter how solid the objectives or relevant the material.

Confusion

Plans for the new-product introduction included a classic "train-the-trainer" approach to disseminating product information. Professional trainers would be educated on the product and marketing program, and they, in turn, would deliver training programs in their own geographic areas. This model, it was believed, would work especially well in Europe, where European trainers could conduct product training in their home countries in their native languages. A continuing education consultant was brought in to develop the train-the-trainer program. Everything worked fine until the consultant crossed the Atlantic. Only then did he discover that (1) the product was not going to be available in Europe for another six months, and (2) there were no professional trainers in the European organization for him to train. Further investigation revealed that the product manager had a personal goal of promoting the product to as many people as possible. Since the product manager knew nothing about the training profession, she envisioned a train-the-trainer program as a general product announcement to forty people per session.

Every person involved in planning or implementing a training program has a vision of what the program is designed to do and of how that vision should become a reality. Unfortunately, people often assume that others share their vision. Unclarified assumptions lead to confusion and pain where training is concerned. Unless purpose, objectives, personal agendas, focus, target audience, and so on are clarified in the planning process, they will act like time bombs ticking away as the program unfolds.

A cautionary note: Sometimes our collaborative zeal can be our downfall. Another continuing educator, diligently working as an internal consultant, ended up with so many levels of management involved in the planning process that by the time training day arrived, there were at least four different management agendas to address. The training session lost its focus, and participants left the session confused, each with a different sense of what they were supposed to do. If we are not clear about what we want participants to learn, how do we expect them to be clear?

Lack of Commitment

From Management. The plan was solid, the training consultant thought. Not only did he have top management support but senior management was actually driving the program. Top management distributed a memorandum to middle managers, telling them about the forthcoming quality assurance training program, and enclosed questionnaires that were supposed to be distributed to employees under each manager's supervision. Results of the questionnaires would be used as the basis for the training program.

Everything worked according to plan until the day of the program. The middle managers, who had been quiet up to that point, started to question the leader on the quality of the data gathered from the questionnaires. Only when the class was in progress did the trainer learn that the managers had quietly subverted the process by distributing the questionnaires to only two employees each. Hence, the data set was too small to be valid. The result was a continuing education program that failed, even with top management support. The moral? Be sure you have commitment from each level of the organization, and if there seem to be inconsistencies in what the various levels expect, negotiate a compromise before planning proceeds.

From Participants. There is a saying among trainers that there are at least three kinds of people in a classroom: prisoners, vacationers, and sponges. One of the challenges continuing educators face is the resistance of "prisoners" and "vacationers" to being in a training session at all. Commitment of participants, first, to being in the room and, second, to learning something is a challenge that planners often overlook and that course leaders must deal with.

Trainers who fail to analyze their audience before the class begins may be unprepared to deal with the following type of exchange between a trainer (me) and a participant:

TRAINER: "Why did you come today?"

PARTICIPANT: "My manager sent me." (I usually respond with "My manager sent me, too, so we have something in common.")

TRAINER: "What is your personal expectation for this training session?"

PARTICIPANT: "I don't expect to get anything out of this class!"

One must plan ways to deal with this kind of resistance. As I quietly hummed a mantra that sounded vaguely like "get me out of here," I reviewed all the possible alternatives. On that day, I sat down, with open body language, and calmly and warmly replied, "Fine. That is certainly your choice." Please note, though, that this kind of response must be practiced and delivered warmly, from the heart and not from the other regions of the body where we generally respond. The truth is that, in my experience, initial resistance and hostility are often a result of fear: fear of exposure (which ironically is often a greater concern for experienced professionals than for novices), fear of wasting time, fear of not getting the right information, fear of generally being vulnerable.

Several years ago a company adopted a specific selling-skills program, and management decreed that every field salesperson had to attend. It was a good idea; it would allow people to develop a common language, create sales plans from the same map, and so on. None of this made much sense, however, to the sales representative who said to me on day one, "I have twenty years of sales experience. Last year I booked $14 million in business. I want to know why I must now spend three days in a basic selling-skills course." Frankly, I didn't know either. I did know that responding "because management said so" would do nothing positive for his attitude or for the atmosphere in the room. We have been taught to "use the expertise of the group," but in this case that would have been patronizing. I asked him to decide for himself what would be worth his time. I later learned that the reason he decided to stay, even for a while, was that the responsibility for his own learning had been pushed back on him. As it turned out, he stayed for the entire course, was a strong contributor, and admitted in the end that it was the first sales training course he had actually ever attended, and he learned a great deal about himself and his style.

Thus, planners and implementors must determine how to gain participants' commitment to the program and how to minimize their fear of being vulnerable, of allowing themselves to participate fully in the learning process. One way to do this is to create a climate of trust so that learning can occur. Participants may begin a program with questions such as "What will you (as the instructor) be reporting about us? And to whom? Will we know what you said? Are we being evaluated here? How? What impact will it have on us after we leave here?" Trainers must agree with the program's sponsor about postcourse feedback requirements and then must address these issues up front in the classroom by telling the participants about any information or assessments related to their participation or performance that will be passed on to others. Set the expectations clearly. If participants do not trust the trainer or are uncertain about what will happen to them as a result of their participation or performance, learning will suffer. And once a "contract of confidentiality" has been struck between the trainer and participant, don't ever be coerced into violating it!

Observers and auditors are people who have found a way to be in the classroom without being fully committed to the process. They usually sit in the back corner, notebook in hand, where they can "just observe." What they are observing is anyone's guess. Course participants generally assume that they are the ones being observed, analyzed, or critiqued and that comments they make will be reported back to their supervisors.

In my experience, there are two types of observers. One is there to learn how to deliver the course: "I really want to observe the process, the instructor, so I'll just sit in the back and take notes. I won't bother anybody." The second doesn't have the time to participate fully in the course but does have the time to sit in: "I would really like to take your course, but I have so much going on right now I really can't commit the time. Do you mind if I just sit in and observe?" I never let anybody "just observe" in my classroom. To the aspiring trainer I say, "The only way to understand how this course comes across is to be a participant in it. If you want to participate in the course two times to understand the process better, that's OK. But you will not be able to determine where and how the course works without participating as an actual learner." To the would-be observer I offer two options: "Make the time to attend the course fully or not at all. Otherwise your revolving-door attendance will interfere with the learning process and will send mixed messages to other participants about the importance of commitment to this program."

Commitment to learning means making the time to be in the classroom by putting other work aside. This is often difficult both for participants and for those they work with. Examples of how easy it is to violate this principle include managers who send their subordinates to training, then continue to interrupt the class, either in person, by telephone, or through time-critical work requirements. "Excuse me, I just need to see Brenda for a minute." "There is another urgent phone message for Bob." "John has to see a customer at 2:00 tomorrow. Will that be a problem?" I sometimes hear from participants, "My manager sent me to this class, but he still expects me to have the proposal to him tomorrow afternoon. I will try to be here for as much as I can, but I am sure you understand . . ."

If any of these sound familiar, consider the issue a planning or implementation oversight. They are all variations on the issue of commitment of managers and participants to the training process.

I am a realist. Work has to be completed. However, continuing educators must make it clear to clients before the training begins that full participation is required in order for the process to be worthwhile.

One way of handling these issues is to state class hours and expectations clearly in a confirmation letter to both participants and their managers. When necessary, send a letter to managers asking them not to disturb anyone during the session and to put aside all other work requirements for participants until after the class is over. This preclass letter or conversation is a good way to screen conflict situations beforehand. If a manager or participant indicates that he or she has time conflicts, agree to reschedule the participant for another offering of the program.

Sounds great, right? What happens, though, when you get to class? As the course leader, you must set an example by living up to your own commitments to the class. You deliver the most critical message on day one: Do you start crisply on time or within fifteen minutes of the start time? After breaks, do you start when you say you will or after everyone returns? If the course leader is sloppy about these things on the first day, it will be difficult to hold anyone else to time commitments.

One trainer was concerned about a seminar for sixty people to be held in New York City. She knew this particular group had a notorious reputation for treating sessions with a revolving-door attitude. People were constantly coming and going from the classroom as they attended to other things that seemed important at the moment. She knew that saying "Sit still" would not work. Instead she said, "We're in New York, so we will treat today's program like an evening at the theater. You each have a copy of today's schedule. If you feel you must leave during any session, please be aware that you will only be permitted to return during the next intermission." Then she lived up to the pledge with the help of an appointed door usher. Results? Terrific. Disruptions reduced by 80 percent. Attention rose significantly. Most important, the formerly disruptive participants thanked her at the end of the day, saying, "At first I thought you were just trying to control us, but I found myself thinking twice before I jumped up to leave in the middle of the session, and I realized that I could allow myself to be here. Consequently, I listened, and I learned today."

From Trainers. Have you ever heard a program leader confess, "I've done this before, and I'm getting bored." In my view, this comment represents a lack of commitment on the part of the trainer. Trainers who lack commitment become dangerously self-centered, rather than learner-centered. I find it curious that any trainer could perceive training experiences as repetitive: Each audience is unique, with individual needs and concerns. Certainly, one becomes familiar with typical questions and recurring issues. Yet any learning that takes place is always unique. I have delivered some programs more than seventy-five times, and, honestly, each time feels like a brand-new experience. Trainers who assume audience A is the same as audience B are making a big mistake.

Another type of trainer attitude problem shows up as "me expert, you peon." One program conducted by a "me expert" trainer resulted in such total intimidation of participants that after the first day no one dared ask a question or make a comment. The one student who did challenge the trainer was so swiftly put in his place that a colleague slipped him a picture of a target with a note that read, "Wear this."

After the course, the trainer reported to management that the program had gone smoothly. Correct. But did learning occur? Definitely. Participants learned to obey. Was that what they were supposed to learn? No, not in the opinion of their supervisors who expected to see them work in a different way. True commitment to participant learning requires us as trainers to put aside our own egos, our personal agendas, and sometimes our beliefs and desires, no matter how well intended.

Another example of the trainer's lack of commitment to participant learning can be summed up in this self-assessment: "The program was a success. They liked me." But evidence that participants liked the trainer or the program is not the same as evidence that they learned. The two are often confused. It is easy to build a program that people will like. Good food, fun and games, entertainment—all make for an enjoyable experience. But some trainers get carried away with the need to be liked. I have seen people sacrifice learning in order to be appealing.

When I met Ned, a corporate trainer with fifteen years' experience and rave reviews, he told me he was actually a frustrated stand-up comic. When I attended Ned's class, I could see that, more than anything else, he needed to be liked. His classes were fun and funny. But Ned's need to be liked interfered with his role as educator. He avoided challenging participants, skipped over the difficult exercises, told many jokes, and used food and gimmicks to get attention and reward correct responses. Please do not misunderstand. I believe learning can and should be interesting, enlightening, and fun. And everyone wants to be liked. But the danger comes when we begin to sacrifice the learning process to meet our own needs.

Lack of Clarity and Courage

A lack of clarity and courage on the part of program planners can lead to the mistakes that prevent participants from learning what planners want them to learn. Clarity and courage are intertwined. A friend of mine once said, right out of the blue, "To act when the moment presents itself is the confluence of clarity and courage." This means having the courage to say Yes to a different approach or new idea, a willingness to take risks to help people find ways to learn for themselves. Sometimes it means sensing you are being led astray by your client and having the courage to say No. Beware the hidden agenda. If you sense one, it is time to summon clarity and courage, and, as my friend said, "Conflue!"

A team development facilitator was caught in a client dilemma and decided to do just that. She was meeting with the senior vice president of a Fortune 500 corporation to outline plans for the forthcoming team development session that was to involve the VP and those who reported to him. The VP told the facilitator that he wanted her to audiotape the session secretly, ostensibly for the record. In fact, the VP's plan was to use the tapes for a performance review that he would soon conduct with a difficult subordinate. The facilitator refused, incurring the wrath of the determined and vocal VP, who was, as we have noted, her client. The VP insisted that the taping be done. A test of wills ensued. With courage and clarity, the facilitator stuck to her guns, stating clearly her reasons for refusing, and no taping was done. I suppose it goes without saying that if the facilitator had agreed to tape the session, even overtly, it would have seriously compromised the learning climate.

Sometimes we say yes when we should say no because we believe in "experts" more than in our own instincts. A major computer company developed a new-hire training program to train college graduates to become successful computer salespeople. Curriculum developers listened to subject matter experts (SMEs) who had been in the computer industry for many years. The SMEs, brilliant computer engineers and computer sales representatives, said the recently hired college graduates must learn assembler language in order to understand computers and be able to talk to customers about them. Assembler language? OK, whatever the SMEs say. So, against the curriculum developers' better judgment, they developed a course in assembler language. It turned out to be a waste of precious time in the training experience. The new employees needed to learn about the marketplace, the businesses of potential customers, and how computer products can be used by the customer. There may have been a time when understanding assembler language was useful, but the market had changed and so had sales requirements.

Why didn't they learn what we wanted them to learn in this case? Because the content had little meaning and application in their world. Developers should have asked more questions and investigated more thoroughly during planning in order to be clear and courageous enough to say no to subject matter experts.

Lack of Cultural Sensitivity

"Bailey, you speak very good English." High praise for a person whose native language is English? You bet. The comment came from a Venezuelan who, like many internationals, had studied English but found that a language studied is different from a language spoken. Why did he offer this compliment? Simple: because he could understand me. The real question is why could I be understood when so many of my English-speaking training colleagues who train internationally cannot? Because many people forget to keep the following rules in mind when speaking to an international audience:

Native English speakers are frequently lazy speakers, often running words together. (Huh? Watya gonna do bout that anyway?) Thus, *Rule Number One* is to speak slowly and clearly and articulate fully, so your listeners can hear each individual word.

I was sure that Hans, from Switzerland, was the most interested student I had encountered in months, because he never took his eyes off me. What a quest for learning! I thought. When I told Hans how impressed I was with his concentrated attention, he laughed and said, "Bailey, I am just reading your lips!" Thus, *Rule Number Two* is to keep your face toward your audience as much as possible. Push out those words. No mumbling allowed. If you concentrate on eye contact with your audience and articulate your words, it will all work out fine. Just don't be put off by the glassy-eyed gaze of your group.

In Germany, I conducted an exercise that was designed to force participants to make changes in their answers. When I asked them what changes they had made, they said none. "None?" I was confused. I knew this group had indeed made several. Rather than confront them, I asked the question another way: "What did you do as a result of this exercise?"

"We modified our responses in three areas."

The next day, in the next exercise debrief, I asked, "Did you make any modifications today?"

"Yes, several," they easily reported.

Rule Number Three, then, is to listen to the word choices, grammar, and syntax that international participants use, and match your words and grammar to theirs.

Here's another example of this rule: When I listened carefully to Jean-Pierre, a French student, he described his father's profession by saying, "Teaching is the career of my father." I compared these words to my own. In English, we use many possessive expressions, "Teaching is my father's job," and contractions, "My father's a teacher." These may be confusing to people for whom English is a second language, especially if they are not around English-speaking people every day. When I said in the class after that, "Is this the book of Jean-Pierre?," four people quickly answered my question. Earlier I had asked, "Is this Jean-Pierre's book?" and had received some blank looks.

You can also heighten understanding by demonstrating words and concepts as much as possible. When I used the term *drafting* to describe the way promotions occur in an organization, the internationals did not know what I meant. I picked up two boxes, put one behind the other, and demonstrated the air pull that automobile drivers experience when following another car or truck closely. That is called drafting. In organizations, when a manager gets promoted, others who work closely with that manager also get pulled along, or drafted. "Ahhhhh," they replied, understanding at last. Thus, *Rule Number Four* is to show and tell.

Find as many common-denominator references as possible. Movies and television shows are excellent examples, since many are shown around the world. In one international session, we were discussing "power plays" in organizations, but my audience did not understand what I meant by the term *power play*. I tried to describe it and offered definitions and examples, all in vain. Finally I asked, "Have you ever seen the television show 'Dallas?'"

"Yes! J. R. Ewing!" they exclaimed. Suddenly all was clear. *Rule Number Five*, then, is to relate through common examples.

As a trainer in a foreign country, you represent your country as well as your organization. You will probably be dealing with some prejudices as a result of the sins of your predecessors. Watch. Observe. Listen. Do some research on the country before you go. Read up on world events (Americans have a dreadful reputation for being poorly informed about world events). When you arrive in the host country, read the local English-language newspaper. The *International Herald Tribune* is available in many countries and is reliable in its news reporting. Other local papers may be available in English, too. Don't talk about "life back home" unless you are asked. Try to meet with local organizational representatives. Plan to spend a day in the local office if you can, to get an understanding of the concerns, customs, and expectations of your client. Even if you have been briefed by the organization's headquarters, it is imperative that you check out your information with the local office. Each of these activities will help establish your credibility and the credibility of the program.

While you're at it, verify local customs for things like lunch. For one of my sessions, the Paris office had made all the logistical arrangements. It was a tight program, needing every second of class time. Proud of myself for running right on schedule, I said to the group, "It's now 12:30. We will break for lunch and begin again promptly at 1:30." They smiled politely. Then we all proceeded to the dining room where a five-course gourmet feast, including three kinds of wine, awaited us. I soon learned this was normal lunch fare for the French, who consider lunch the major meal of the day. I mentally rearranged my program schedule as each delicious course was served, all the while composing *Rule Number Six*: Learn as much as you can ahead of time about the country and the specific organization where you will be training.

Conclusion

"Why didn't they learn what we wanted them to learn?" boils down to a question of expectations. Programs are designed to accomplish certain outcomes. Sponsors and participants both have expectations about what will be learned in a program. Planners and instructors have the obligation to design and deliver an educational experience that will meet the expectations of all stakeholders. This chapter has addressed a number of factors that may explain why participants didn't learn what we wanted them to learn and has offered suggestions about how to improve the likelihood that expected outcomes will be achieved. But this analysis would not be complete without viewing the question from one more perspective.

One of the major barriers to learning can be lack of agreement between the educator and learners about what is to be learned. Learners are free to decide what they wish to learn, regardless of the desires, expectations, or hopes of others. Education can be imposed, but learning cannot. As Phill Wilson of Alliance Associates in Chapel Hill, North Carolina, has said, "After all the planning is done, I simply try to provide a climate that will allow learning to occur. When I begin a session I tell people, 'I am here to help you find things that are useful to you, to help you find ways to apply these concepts to your own environment, perhaps to reorganize your toolbox.' What people leave the class with is probably different for each person, and that's OK, because what they leave with is not *my* toolbox, but theirs" (Phill Wilson, personal communication, June 1990).

The intent of this chapter has been to identify some of the factors that account for participants' lack of learning. Although learning itself is under the control of the learner, our challenge as continuing educators is to create an environment and forms of interaction that facilitate learning. Successfully meeting this challenge requires care, commitment, clarity, courage, and cultural sensitivity. The anecdotes presented here describe a variety of mistakes and the lessons that can be learned from them. Applying these lessons to the design and delivery of instruction should increase the chances that program outcomes will match our intentions.

P. Bailey Allard of Allard Associates, Chapel Hill, North Carolina, is a professional development trainer and consultant with extensive international experience.

Understanding why learning is not applied in participants' natural environments can lead to the design of more effective education and training programs.

Understanding the Application of Learning

Richard W. Kemerer

People will learn anything if their lives depend on it, says Mager (1975). Perhaps the key to the application of learning resides in the learner's perception of how important the new learning is to his or her ability to work effectively in the setting where the application must take place.

This chapter provides some insights about what prevents the application of learning and what can be done to increase the chances that new learning will be applied once learners return to their natural environments. The reader should be cautioned, however, that although I consider myself an adult educator, these insights are colored by the context in which I work, which is largely business and industry.

My view of the educational process was substantially influenced by Knowles's (1980) *The Modern Practice of Adult Education: From Pedagogy to Andragogy;* Gagné's (1977) *The Conditions of Learning;* Mager's (1975) *Preparing Instructional Objectives;* Bloom's (1956) *Taxonomy of Educational Objectives, Handbook 1: The Cognitive Domain;* Harlow's (1949) "The Development of Learning Sets"; and Skinner's (1969) *Contingencies of Reinforcement: A Theoretical Analysis.* It was not until I was asked to design training programs for literally thousands of employees doing the same job or to help corporations get a handle on hooking all training efforts into corporate strategic objectives that I added McClelland, Atkinson, Clark, and Lowell's (1953) *The Achievement Motive* and Herzberg's (1966) *Work and the Nature of Man* to my list.

Herzberg is important in understanding the transfer of learning because he proposed that people will put in the effort to perform well in their natural environment if they see the connection between their perfor-

NEW DIRECTIONS FOR ADULT AND CONTINUING EDUCATION, no. 49, Spring 1991 ©Jossey-Bass Inc., Publishers

mance and a meaningful reward. Like Skinner, Herzberg felt that the reward, or the perception of reward, pulls behavior: Identify the right reward, connect it to the right behavior, and you have a complete system. McClelland, Atkinson, Clark, and Lowell (1953) proposed that all people want to master their environment successfully and that this is a major motivator.

For most people, learning is only a means to an end. Effective educators understand this, and they design programs that show how learning can be applied, or transferred, from an "unnatural" classroom setting or training session to the actual setting where the learner works. Knowles (1980) and Gagné (1977) suggest that if transfer is to take place, the learning environment must resemble as much as possible the environment in which the learning will be applied.

Think about the best teachers you have had. What made them so special? My guess is that they connected with you; they spoke to where you were at that particular point in your experience. They seemed to understand and put into your learning environment what you needed to know and do in order for you to master the environment outside of the classroom.

In business and industry, every employee performs certain functions and tasks that are linked together in various jobs, whose outputs are required in order for the corporation to produce something of value. The best companies, like the best teachers, connect with their employees, applying the theories of the great educators, psychologists, and organizational behaviorists to the work environment.

Great companies make the transfer of learning almost seamless because the work environment and the learning environment are one and the same. These companies connect three key components under the label of "performance management." For every employee, they answer three questions clearly:

1. What am I supposed to do all day long?
2. How can I get better at it?
3. What will be my reward for doing my job right?

The best companies have actually reduced the hours of classroom training time by moving the training to where the employee works. They have also created a supportive work environment where the employee and supervising manager work together to ensure that answers to the three questions listed here are never in doubt.

Here is an example to illustrate what happens when corporations assume that the linkages among these three key questions are unimportant. One company, world famous in the financial industry, commissioned our firm to clarify the answers to the three key questions for employees in several revenue-generating positions. We conducted an employee self-assessment to identify what each employee felt were the most important tasks in his or her job and what kind of further development was needed—whether that development consisted of additional training, more supervision, or better communication. The results were spectacular—not to the employees but to the executives. First, we discovered that the total employee population was unclear about executives' expectations for their jobs. Second, despite several expensive and well-designed training programs aimed at these employees, there was seemingly no transfer of learning from the programs to the job. Finally, the truth was discovered: There was no reward mechanism. In executives' haste to communicate and train employees about new job requirements, they had neglected to change the reward system. The employees knew that there was no real motivation for them to make changes.

In the business world, responses to the three questions are worked out jointly between the company and the individual employee. In the public sector, perhaps the onus is more on the individual to ask the questions and reach reasonable answers privately.

Factors Inhibiting Learning Transfer

The specific factors that become impediments to the application of learning can be organized according to the same three questions.

Structuring Expectations. Six common mistakes account for the difficulty in reaching agreement about what people are expected to do in their work.

Lack of Clarity. Are the expectations that apply in the natural environment clear? As I have pointed out, they may not be, even though a company has made efforts to "communicate." But even if one is retiring from an active work environment to a less active one, he or she must be clear about the behaviors needed to adjust successfully to this changing role for learning transfer to occur.

Focus on Knowledge, Not Behavior. I suspect that one of the greatest inhibiting factors to my own transfer of learning to the work world was that I spent hundreds of hours sitting in classrooms and libraries *learning* rather than *doing*. And one of the reasons that universities have had to scramble for funding in the last ten years is that many people no longer buy the myth that knowledge automatically leads to application. Similarly, unless performance expectations for participants in adult education are set out in terms of specific behaviors, there will be little or no transfer of learning.

Poor Timing. Havighurst and Orr (1956), Knowles (1980), and others have argued at length about readiness as a key variable in learning. There can be little doubt that without the perception by the learner of the need for new behaviors, there is no motivation to change and therefore no readiness to learn. Thus, the introduction of new or changed work expectations has to be timed carefully so that participants are ready to learn when the training program is offered.

Expectations Not Possible or Doable. Perhaps the required behavioral changes are too great for many people. All the good intentions in the world will not achieve unrealistic expectations. I once worked as a student counselor at a vocational and technical college of further education in Australia. I remember one young adult who could not spell well but wanted to become an engineer. He thought he could complete successfully the engineering part of his schooling but felt he would have a hard time with the written part of the various courses he would have to take. My role was to help him assess whether he could make it through the course requirements. As all good psychologists would, I presented him with a barrage of tests, one of which examined his visual, fine-motor coordination. As he began to draw the various pictures, I could not help but notice that he drew everything perfectly (he was employed as a cake decorator) but that his visual field was ninety degrees off. In other words, he saw what you and I see only when he tilted his head sideways. Counseling him into a more realistic occupation seemed required.

Expectations Changed. We live in a rapidly changing world, so much so that stability of expectations is as much a factor as the expectations themselves. One way to ensure that learning transfer will not occur easily is to shift requirements in the natural environment so rapidly that one never gets the chance to focus on expected behavior. Certainly, one of the biggest challenges in business and industry is to focus early on short-term expectations while leaving room for long-term change. In some industries, the short term may be only three months. This does not leave much time to ensure that employees are clear on their various roles and responsibilities.

No Ownership. Perhaps the greatest inhibiting factor related to expectations occurs when the intended performers—the people themselves—are not involved in developing those expectations. As a public sector adult education practitioner, I was once asked to conduct a workshop on needs assessment for continuing education and public school adult education program administrators in a large city. This particular city set aside a substantial fund for creative programs, and this money was available as long as a need had been established. I noticed that nearly 50 percent of the funding was being spent on disco dancing courses for the elderly. When asked, the workshop attendees argued that because of the large number of "shut-ins" (elderly persons living in condominiums) in the area, such courses provided social as well as physical rewards—even though a relatively small percentage of the total community benefited or attended.

I suggested that a needs assessment involving a broad spectrum of the community might serve to validate the need for such programs. Accepting my challenge, they orchestrated a multitude of collection methods and analysis techniques—with the cooperation of churches, newspapers, and radio stations. I noticed soon after the results came back that the disco courses disappeared and were replaced by programs that responded to more of the community's overall needs.

I suspect what happened was that the practitioners, as providers of programs, assumed that they knew what the community's needs were. Only when the community spoke did the true needs surface.

The point I am making is covered in the word *ownership*. Companies that fail to listen to their employees have a much more difficult time gaining their commitment and continuous improvement than do companies that involve their employees in structuring personal objectives around the bigger, corporate objectives. Similarly, continuing education programs that do not tie into broad community needs will not see much transfer of learning occur for their participants.

Improving Skills. The second question (How can I get better at my work?) indicates that some of the key variables impeding learning transfer are related to the design and implementation of training programs, while others concern the reinforcement after training provided by the managing supervisor and peer group.

Unfocused Learning Objectives. One of the best ways I know to inhibit the transfer of learning is to use learning objectives that (1) are written from the instructor's, not the learner's, point of view, (2) are so specific that they sound odd, and (3) do not mirror the exact tasks required by a job.

Objectives written from the instructor's point of view look something like this: "Introduce learners to the concept of financial analysis through the use of ratios." These objectives do not specify what the learner will be able to do after taking the course. In short, they focus on teaching method rather than on learning outcome.

One training department with nearly a hundred trainers on staff was asked to gear up for new programs. Their company's chairperson had announced that he was bringing in over a hundred MBAs from leading universities each year for five years, thereby injecting new blood and skills into the organization. At the time, no high-profile development program existed, and the training department's task was to put one together. Because of short time lines, staff members decided to bundle some of the shorter, existing training courses together to make up a comprehensive intake program.

It is easy to imagine what happened. Much of the existing training exemplified the worst training design and practices known. One major flaw was that each learning objective was written from the instructor's point of view, thus focusing on teaching rather than on learning. These objectives needed to answer the question, "What will the participant be able to *do* after the course?"

The instructional designers rewrote the objectives but insisted on using the three-part format (conditions, behavior, and criteria) promoted by Mager (1975), making the outcomes of learning sound so odd that no one could figure out what they meant. The result of this redrafting exercise was a program that was not internally consistent or compatible with the business environment.

Finally, unfocused objectives may not specify the exact tasks required. A friend of mine, for example, signed up for the radio corps in the army because he was interested in electronics and was told he would get an opportunity to "work on" radios. He ended up painting, dusting, and cleaning radios—not at all what he had expected. Ambiguity in learning objectives may thus be useful for recruiting purposes, but it can also create major obstacles to the transfer of learning to participants' actual job tasks.

Objectives at the Incorrect Level of the Cognitive Domain. Pretend for the moment that you are going to teach me how to negotiate a sales closing meeting in my new job as an account manager for a financial institution. Bloom (1956) divided the cognitive domain of learning into several levels of increasing complexity: knowledge, comprehension, application, analysis, synthesis, and evaluation. The knowledge level would be exemplified by my being able to state the principles of negotiation or to recall basic negotiating steps. Explaining why they are necessary would be an example of the comprehension level. Actually demonstrating how to negotiate would illustrate the application level. I often find training programs are twice as long as they need to be, with too much time spent on knowledge and comprehension and too little time on application. Courses that assume that participants will be able to apply new learning merely because they know and understand that new learning make an inferential leap that inhibits transfer. This leap is similar to the proposal that one can lose weight or quit smoking simply by understanding the negative effects of obesity or of carcinogens on the body.

Too Many Cooks in the Kitchen. A common problem in most large companies spread out over great geographical distances is "fiddling." Some group somewhere in the organization (usually corporate training) builds a fantastic program based on corporate need. Once built, the program goes out into the corporation's world where someone else (usually a line manager some distance away from headquarters or someone in a regional training center) "fiddles" with the program: That person deletes sections B and C, adds another day on some other topic, and so on. In essence, the program that the corporate group felt was effective because it was designed to meet corporate needs was later "redesigned" by regional groups because they felt it did not meet their regional needs. What is distressing is that both groups are right, but they usually don't communicate well.

Possible results of "fiddling" include poor application of adult education principles, an overall approach that is too heavily wedded to the class-room, the use of computer-based instruction when it is not appropriate, a fixation on some one methodology, or a program that becomes isolated from the real world of problem solving and application. All of these results can lead to poor learning transfer.

Unit of Change Too Small or Inappropriate. Those of us who were lucky enough to learn about the adoption-diffusion curve (Rogers, 1983) have noticed that most training is aimed at the individual learner. This means that, in essence, we participate in a program because we, individually, want to improve a skill. In the work environment, we go back to our unit pumped full of new knowledge and skills, only to find that our colleagues who have not yet attended the course are happily performing their job functions in the old way. You only have to know a little about social psychology to predict that we would rather fit into our social work group (and be invited to lunch on Fridays) than apply new learning by ourselves. Thus, program planners would be far wiser to use the entire work unit, rather than the individual employee, as the unit of change. Some successful organizations apply this technique as part of "pilot tests" in a smaller part of the total system, like a single retail outlet or a branch office.

Adult education theory tells us that the greater the gap between the ideal situation and the actual situation, the greater the need. Thus, individuals who are farthest away from the ideal performance are often the first selected to participate in training programs. But experience and research suggest that this is not a good principle to follow if large-scale change is the desired outcome. As Rogers (1983) predicted years ago, in order to get a critical mass of change among many people, the first target group should be the influential few, the good communicators, and, I hasten to add, those who most likely do not require any training.

The reason for this is that application of new skills or behaviors is risky. There is comfort in stability, due largely to predictability. But when whole systems change, most individuals will adopt a wait-and-see attitude, letting the early adopters forge ahead in uncharted waters. Thus, the transfer of new learning into the natural environment is more difficult for individuals than for groups, and it is less successful if aimed at middle and late adopters than at those bold few who can influence the total group.

Training Isolated. Most companies have found out the hard way that the "garage approach" to skill development not only is expensive but is of limited value. In the "garage approach," employees go away from their work setting to the "training garage" to get fixed. Of course, while they are away, their desks pile high with work that someone else grudgingly contends with, creating a negative backlash to training. The more successful companies have integrated training into the work units under the supervision of a manager or coordinator who makes policies concerning space, time, and pay issues. Thus, the informal network of learning and skill transfer is enhanced, and the formal training system is seen as a different tool rather than as the only tool.

Have you ever wondered how people learn all there is to know that is necessary for functioning in today's world? I suspect that this informal, modeling approach is the prevailing means by which transfer occurs, rather than formal training systems.

Establishing Rewards. Many of us obtain reinforcement from intrinsic rewards, such as personal satisfaction and transfer of skills, and these are strong enough to sustain our new performance level. For instance, we are rewarded by being able to wire a new room or house we are building after completing an electrical wiring course. Rewards can also be extrinsic. A few key factors about rewards stand out that affect transfer.

Little Reinforcement on the Job. Without the application and reinforcement of new skills, new behaviors are likely to diminish. In business, the supervisor is a key factor in reinforcement. Horror stories abound about how one succeeding management level unwittingly undoes what was learned by another. In essence, the supervising level becomes the major obstacle to transfer. In large companies, the participant's finger often points upward with the comment, "I shouldn't be in this program; my boss should be here." One company developed and implemented a management development program for first-line supervisors. At the end of the first year, the company listened to this finger-pointing comment and the following year offered the same program to second-line supervisors. I was talking to one of the executives a year later who was still hearing the same comment. He said to me with a wink, "Well, they're getting closer to the real problem."

My point is that transfer of skills in the work environment requires reinforcement by the immediate supervisor. More important, in multilayered complex organizations transfer of skills requires total vertical integration where one succeeding management level reinforces the behaviors of subordinate levels. The best way to ensure failure is to start at the lowest level rather than at the top and work down.

Delayed Application. I remember one situation where every secretary was sent to a computer course because a company wanted to upgrade their word-processing technology. Groups of employees were selected on the basis of when their unit would be using the new technology; then they participated in a well-designed and well-executed training program. Unfortunately, the arrival of their new computers was delayed six months, so when the employees returned to their workstations, both their heightened expectations and their newly learned skills diminished quickly. If we don't wire our house soon after completing our wiring course, we will naturally forget how to do it.

Economic Rewards Do Not Match New Skills. In the business world, employees are rewarded economically for applying skills. Just about the best way to ensure no transfer of skills after a training program is to fail to reward the desired behaviors. A case in point: One large financial institution wanted to improve its management practices. The initial approach to developing a curriculum was to conduct a needs assessment involving over a thousand managers at all levels who rank-ordered twenty-five management tasks such as planning, delegating, controlling, and so forth. For each task, managers assessed how important the task was to their success, what further development they needed, and the degree to which they were rewarded.

Results showed three lists of ranked management tasks (importance, training, and reward). Of particular interest was number 25, budgeting, which the consensus of managers ranked on the bottom in terms of importance and skill development but on top in terms of reward. Here was an organization where the reward system undid its own management system and, as it turned out, its training system. Managers knew how to do important management tasks but were rewarded more if they concentrated on some of the least important tasks.

Reward Delay. A final factor affecting the success of learning transfer is the immediacy of reward. When I ride a bicycle correctly after my riding course, I am immediately rewarded because I have mastered my environment. Often in business and industry, rewards are so far removed from the desired performance that they are ineffective. Companies that place their emphasis on performance appraisal as a once-a-year form-filling-out procedure and then delay bonuses or commissions for up to six months are missing one of the strongest reinforcers in transfer. Much wiser would be an approach that emphasizes day-to-day, informal feedback by supervisors and market-oriented results.

Strategies for Increasing Learning Transfer

Figure 1 illustrates how to maximize transfer of learning in one's natural environment and presents a shorthand list of the factors described in this section. We can use Figure 1 as an action plan for increasing learning transfer. Although much of my own experience and the examples I have used have come from the private sector, I suggest that this plan can also apply directly to the work of my colleagues in the public sector.

Structuring Expectations

Clarify Expectations. Use imaging skills to develop clear pictures of ideal behaviors. Focus on what participants in an educational activity should be able to do better after their attendance. Allow time for discussion by participants on how a particular educational experience links to their world.

Break down complex functions into simpler components or tasks. Sometimes it is difficult for us to see the steps that lead to broader achievements.

Figure 1. How to Enhance Transfer

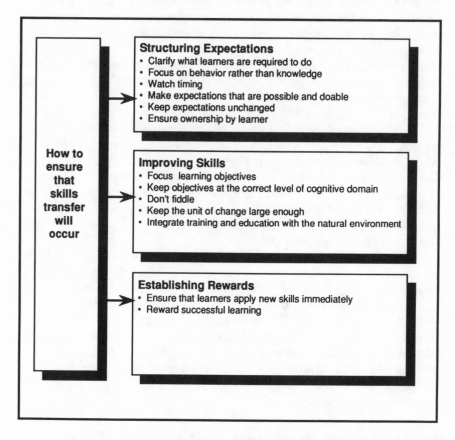

Structuring Expectations
- Clarify what learners are required to do
- Focus on behavior rather than knowledge
- Watch timing
- Make expectations that are possible and doable
- Keep expectations unchanged
- Ensure ownership by learner

Improving Skills
- Focus learning objectives
- Keep objectives at the correct level of cognitive domain
- Don't fiddle
- Keep the unit of change large enough
- Integrate training and education with the natural environment

Establishing Rewards
- Ensure that learners apply new skills immediately
- Reward successful learning

How to ensure that skills transfer will occur

You should help participants recognize the relationship between the capabilities they are developing and the work they are expected to do.

Be as specific as you need to be so that others see the same behaviors as you when you describe them. Often we are not as clear as we think we are in explaining our expectations to others. A good rule of thumb is to err on the side of being too specific rather than too general. Focus training on manageable short-term changes that build toward longer-term objectives. Demonstrate to participants how what they learn today and apply tomorrow can lead to the attainment of their larger goals.

Focus on Behavior. Use action verbs to describe required behaviors—for example, calculating, discriminating, and identifying, rather than knowing and understanding. Tie programs to specific tasks that participants will do after they return to their natural environments.

Focus on the Short Term. Focus on the next three months, not a lifetime; otherwise, expectations seem insurmountable and "demotivating."

Ambition is a valued trait in our society, but it must be tempered with realism. Offering programs that try to do too much will be disappointing to the provider and frustrating to the participants. Ensure that the expectations of all concerned are realistic. Motivate for the next hurdle, not the last.

Ensure Doability. Make sure that both individual and corporate expectations are realistic. Don't try to turn the aircraft carrier around in less than three miles of open sea—it's not doable. As a future participant, what can you actually achieve in terms of new behaviors, given your makeup and other demands? Do you want to lose a pound a week or three? Do you want to take a short sail on a weekend or sail to Hawaii? As program designers, what needs in your community can you effectively address—illiteracy of the entire city or of a targeted population within the city?

Determine Fixed Expectations. Identify several key expectations that are not likely to change in the short term. Design computer programs to teach skills that will still be required over the next three to six months rather than for an application that will be out of date in three to six months. As a future participant, differentiate fixed needs from shifting ones.

Focus instruction first on *what* participants are expected to do and then on *how* they are expected to do it, since the "whats" in life change less often than the "hows."

Instill Ownership. Allow for participation in setting expectations. In the private sector, to dictate expectations to employees without their involvement will find you charging up the hill all alone. In the public sector, the individual is often left to his or her own devices to set expectations. Those of us in counseling roles should take special care to ensure that those we counsel own their goals and expectations.

Improving Skills

Focus Learning Objectives on Behaviors. Leave the heavy verbiage to the academics and use simple, everyday language. Program designers should write their objectives in language understandable to the intended participants. One of the clearest statements I have heard about a course's results was the phrase "Bunetics—tighten those buns!" There is no doubt in my mind about the intended outcome.

Allow participants to adapt program objectives to their own personal objectives. This recommendation is particularly important for program facilitators. Often programs have been built on "macro" needs or "gaps" that a population experiences in skill levels. Actual participants sitting in your classroom on day one of your program may not feel the same need as the general population. To ensure that your participants understand and accept your program's learning objectives, allow at least thirty minutes for participants to adapt program objectives to their real needs. A few minutes set aside at the outset can greatly enhance learning transfer.

Focus on Application. Focus on attainable behaviors in the learning environment. Facilitate realistically. If your program calendar states that participants will be able to write an opera by the time they complete your course (using the piano under their seat), ensure that they can do so (and that there is a piano under their seat!).

Allow time for application in the learning environment with plenty of feedback and reinforcement. Often one of the most difficult challenges program facilitators face is to fill the hours of a class with meaningful activity. Perhaps the most meaningful activity is to allow participants to practice new behaviors and receive feedback on their progress. A course on electrical wiring should allow adequate time for wiring a three-way switch.

Use Efficient and Effective Methodology. Allow for a minimum of 60 percent active participation during a course or program. Active participation means that the participants, not the facilitator, talk. In any class with adult participants, there is a substantial experience base represented among the participants. Use it.

Provide practice in application through the use of case studies and frequent feedback. Case studies reflect real situations and have been proven to promote integration of learning. Sometimes, participants can develop their own case studies, giving them to fellow students.

Use multiple approaches—such as computer-based instruction, video-based instruction, and printed materials for self-study—to teach the same content. Not all of us learn through our eyes or ears. To enhance the integration of new content, use multiple means. Allowing participants to share their experience, for example, adds to the learning of others and enables each participant to "hook" new learning to their own experience.

Build training programs so that they can be adapted to fit the specific situation and group of participants. Accept the fact that given geographical or other perceived distance, the human being will mold programs to his or her needs. Program designers should allow for certain changes that do not affect the pedagogy of the program.

Focus on the Larger Unit. As much as possible, focus change on one's social or work unit, rather than on the individual. As one of my colleagues said, "I would like the unit of change in my organization to be nothing smaller than the numbers required to fill a baseball stadium." This is obviously impossible for a continuing education course open to the general public. But, for those of us involved in promoting adult education concepts in the community, it is quite possible to work with education boards or community groups where the level of change is the entire board or group.

Make Training and Education Part of the Natural Environment. Emphasize the informal, natural network of learning as much as possible. Rather than filling every moment of your program with intensive activities, allow for informal learning occurrences such as breaks. Those of us who attend conferences regularly would probably agree that we learn as much outside the formal sessions as in them.

In the business environment, focus on well-written policies and procedures supplemented with job aids to form the basic foundation for learning job tasks, rather than on formal courses.

Again, in the business environment, ensure that supervisors are equipped with enough tools and knowledge to train employees on the job, rather than send them away to some other part of the organization for learning.

Reward

Encourage Application of New Skills. Encourage participants to apply new skills as soon as possible. Successful application is its own reward and will reinforce the learning.

In business and industry, supervisors should provide a work environment that allows for the application of new skills directly when employees return from a training program. This means that new equipment, if needed, is in the work unit when they return.

Provide Rewards. Alter previously outdated reward systems that go against the transfer of new learning. For example, if your educational program teaches nutrition and weight control, do not suggest that participants reward themselves for each day of self-control with chocolate cake.

Make rewards meaningful. If the most an employee can gain by successfully meeting expectations is a 2 percent increase in annual salary (which will be all but eaten up by increased taxes), the reward system will be ineffective.

Conclusion

This chapter presents a picture from my experience of what seems to enhance skills transfer. There are three simple questions your adult students are asking: What behaviors do I want to improve? How can training and education help me? What's in it for me if I actually do improve my behavior?

One of my mentors cautions, "If I only knew what I wanted, life would be a simple matter." Helping adult learners clarify what they want to achieve in their natural environment is no easy task. Clarity at the outset of an educational activity is, however, one of the key elements to skills transfer because it links rewards to improved skills. Without clear goals, any educational activity will be acceptable, but only limited transfer will result.

I started my educational career as a part-time secondary school teacher in a rough school in Australia. At the start of my first day, I asked my curriculum adviser what I needed to do to be successful. His answer was simply, "Get through to them. I don't care whether you use any of the books in the book room or not." I survived that year because, like you, I listened to my students' needs and matched the educational activities to the new behaviors required of them. I encourage you to model the best teacher you ever had. Chances are that he or she connected with where you wanted to go, helped you get there, and rewarded you accordingly—and you transferred your new learning to your environment without even thinking about it.

References

Bloom, B. S. (ed.). *Taxonomy of Educational Objectives, Handbook 1: Cognitive Domain.* New York: McKay, 1956.
Gagné, R. M. *The Conditions of Learning.* (3rd ed.) New York: Holt, Reinhart & Winston, 1977.
Harlow, H. F. "The Development of Learning Sets." *Psychological Review,* 1949, *56,* 51–65.
Havighurst, R. J., and Orr, B. *Adult Education and Adult Needs.* Chicago: Center for the Study of Liberal Education for Adults, 1956.
Herzberg, F. *Work and the Nature of Man.* Cleveland, Ohio: World Publishing, 1966.
Knowles, M. S. *The Modern Practice of Adult Education: From Pedagogy to Andragogy.* (Rev. ed.) Chicago: Follett, 1980.
McClelland, D. C., Atkinson, J. W., Clark, R. A., and Lowell, E. L. *The Achievement Motive.* East Norwalk, Conn.: Appleton-Century-Crofts, 1953.
Mager, R. F. *Preparing Instructional Objectives.* (2nd ed.) Belmont, Calif.: Fearon, 1975.
Rogers, E. M. *The Diffusion of Innovations.* (3rd ed.) New York: Free Press, 1983.
Skinner, B. F. *Contingencies of Reinforcement: A Theoretical Analysis.* East Norwalk, Conn.: Appleton-Century-Crofts, 1969.

Richard W. Kemerer is president of Richard Kemerer and Associates, a performance management consulting firm based in Toronto, Ontario, Canada.

How we cope with feelings of failure determines whether the lessons we learn can be used to achieve success.

Responding to Success and Failure

Helen H. Mills

Failure is defined in the *American Heritage Dictionary of the English Language* as "the condition or fact of not achieving the desired end or ends. One that fails. The consideration or fact of being insufficient or lacking; a falling short; a weakening." Synonyms for failure from Roget's *New Thesaurus* include unsuccess, bomb, bust, dud, lemon, loser, washout, decline, weakening, and breakdown. No wonder we hesitate to talk about failure!

This volume has been designed to help adult and continuing educators understand why programs fail. Programs fail for a variety of reasons, some of which have already been discussed. To paraphrase Murphy's Law, when something *can* go wrong, it *will* go wrong.

Possible reasons for program failure include the fact that attendance was low (marketing didn't work; topic wasn't right or was ahead of its time; time of day, week, or month was wrong); the content wasn't satisfactory (instructor was off track; needs survey didn't reveal a critical topic; group was ahead of or behind the level of content); or the facilities were bad (refreshments weren't ready on time; chairs were hard; rest room wasn't clean; room was too hot or too cold). All these and many more elements can make a program fail regardless of how hard we try as planners. But knowing that failure is occasionally inevitable does not make us feel better about it. This chapter will explore the impact of failure, the feelings that failure can arouse in us, and ways to cope with failure.

Two assumptions undergird all that follows. One is that everyone fails. While it may appear to the outside world that some escape the experience of failure, it simply isn't so. The second assumption is that our ability to take risks is closely tied to our ability to cope with failure and that not taking risks in continuing education will paralyze the profession and our service to others. The development of coping mechanisms for failure is as essential to our ability to develop outstanding continuing education programs as are good program development principles.

The Human Dimension of Failure

Because we are sometimes hesitant to talk about our programming failures, we don't recognize that others, too, experience many of the same emotions that we experience. When was the last time a colleague told you *first* about a programming failure when you met at an annual meeting? I can just hear it now: "Jim, it's so good to see you; it's been a whole year. How are you doing?" "Well, Sue, I just had the most amazing program failure. Let me tell you about it. I spent three months on a needs survey, 200 hours in advisory committee meetings, and $10,000 on marketing, and we had to cancel the program because no one signed up!" Even among colleagues who see each other frequently, failure is not an endearing topic. We generally don't want to hear about people's health problems, and we don't want to hear about their failures either.

Our ability to cope with program failures depends on a number of variables. The frequency of failure, the impact of a failure on overall programming efforts, and the costs of the failure in terms of real money and in terms of relationships are elements that can influence our feelings. Additional reasons such as the perception of others, especially supervisors, and general self-esteem, success or failure notwithstanding, can all have a bearing on how we feel about a program failure. "If you feel you are failing, you need to sift out the validity and lack of it in other people's perceptions of you, and then learn to control how those perceptions affect you" (Grogg, 1983, p. 88).

Campbell (1989) states that "no matter how motivated or hardworking you are in any quest, you will inevitably experience obstacles. How you react to these setbacks and whether or not you perceive them as failures may have been determined in your childhood and by your temperament" (p. 78). Clifford (1979) says that failure can have both detrimental and enhancing effects on individuals. For some, the experience of a failure shapes their resolve and becomes the motivating factor behind creative, energetic, and innovative efforts. For others, failure can cause self-doubt and embarrassment, thereby stymieing future efforts.

Driscoll (1989) identifies four benefits of failure: (1) It makes us tougher, stronger, and more resilient to the struggle; (2) we become more aware of what we are up against; (3) it acts as a stepping-stone to success; and (4) it renews our humility and prevents us from taking ourselves too seriously. But it can be the fear of failure, rather than failure itself, that immobilizes us. Finesilver (1989) talked about the fear of failure in a commencement address at Front Range Community College. The address was titled "The Tapestry of Your Life: Don't Be Afraid to Fail," suggesting that each of us will find success and failure woven together throughout life. Finesilver's message included references to Babe Ruth's strikeout record (1,300 times, more than any other ballplayer of his time) and to the 753 manuscript rejections received by English novelist John Creasy before he published 564 books! These examples remind us that even people we consider successful have experienced failure on the road to their successes. Finesilver says, "Don't worry about failure. My suggestion to each of you: Worry about the chances you miss when you don't even try" (p. 83).

Keller and Mills (1983) wrote that, "as adult and continuing educators, we need to be conscious of the influences of success and failure as we begin to talk to each other concerning program failures. Our focus should not be on condemning each other for failure but on exploring program failure, how it personally affects us, and how we can learn from it" (p. 28).

Since some program failures are almost a guaranteed occurrence for adult and continuing educators and since coping with those failures can require different techniques for different people, let's explore a variety of ways in which one can begin to "recover" from program failures. The techniques outlined are not intended to be applicable to all people; each person may find one or more suggestions to be particularly useful. The list is not exhaustive, but as one looks through the literature on coping with failure, the following thirteen suggestions seem to surface time and again.

Techniques for Coping

Accept Total Blame. Some have the self-assurance and life understanding that it takes to say simply, "I goofed!" This technique emerged from a discussion with a colleague when I asked how he had coped over the years with various program failures. It startled me at first but then began to make sense. He went on to explain: First, take the entire blame for the failure and let those feelings settle in. Next, begin to take the experience apart and figure out which parts you had total control over. For those elements that you did have control over, continue to accept the total blame. But there are probably few elements in the program planning process over which you had total control. For those elements that you didn't have control over, begin to analyze where the control was and let go of the feeling of failure about those elements. In other words, we can afford to share the failure and still retain both a sense of self-worth and regard for everyone in the project. Probably few of the other players in the program planning process had total control either.

Deny the Failure. This is probably the first step that many of us take. It is easier to deny the failure when the program that failed was small or when a failure has only occurred once and the consequences were limited. Sometimes such denial is a realistic response: After all, we don't need to make a mountain out of a molehill! However, it is a dangerous response if, in fact, the reason for the failure is tied to how we do our jobs as continuing educators.

Sometimes we deny a failure by simply calling it something else. Haven't we all said something like "this program was not as successful as we had hoped"? Or "failure is not defeat, it is only an experience that yields less than what we had expected" (Driscoll, 1989)? This type of denial may not be helpful in maintaining our self-esteem and allowing us to learn from the experience. But if the consequences of the failure are severe, we must take the next step in order to recover, going beyond denial to look at causes.

Analyze the Failure. Periodically we need to reexamine our skills as a program planner and our understanding of basic program planning principles. A failed program is a good occasion for conducting a personal audit of our adult education practices. This type of audit may lead us to a new understanding of our own professional development needs in some particular area. Brookfield (1990) describes a process of analyzing "critical incidents." A program failure is one type of critical incident, and analyzing that failure may shed some light on adult education principles that in another context were unclear. For example, you may want to reexamine the goals for which the failed program was designed. In many of our programs we are attempting to effect behavioral change—attitudes, lifestyles, values—and in many cases we have little control over whether the change actually occurs.

If you do spot an area in your professional development that needs work, develop a plan of action for correcting the deficiency. The plan of action may consist of selectively reading or rereading in an area; it may mean seeking out another professional for advice on how he or she has handled a particular programming area; it may require taking a course— any number of responses can help hone our skills. With this technique we are seeking solutions to the failure, rather than excuses.

Blame the Other Person. This, too, is a natural response. Again, if the failure is not too great, the consequences not too dire, and the pattern of failure not too repetitive, this type of response can have a cleansing effect. It may not be true, but it can be cathartic! A word of caution: Don't blame the other person too loudly; he or she may be just the person you need the next time out. This technique is best conducted in your head by means of those wonderful imaginary conversations we all have with other people.

Regardless of where the blame falls, it is important to understand why the failure occurred so that it does not occur again. Thus, blaming others is not a substitute for more positive and proactive responses.

Talk and Share. Carefully chosen people who can be trusted to respect you and your feelings can provide a forum for airing your frustrations, doubts, and questions. Should you be lucky enough to have a mentor, supervisor, friend, or colleague who will allow you the time and space to work through your feelings, you are indeed a fortunate person. We all hope to work in an environment that is supportive, one that can help us separate the feelings of having a program failure from the sense of being a failure. Many of us do work in this type of environment. Some don't. We may have to seek support from people outside of work. The point is that isolating ourselves may reinforce the notion that our program failure is unusual or unique. By talking with trusted people we often learn that our experiences and feelings are ones that others have also worked through and felt. Their sharing with you may provide solutions for dealing with a program failure.

Richard Nixon's (1990) recently published book *In the Arena: A Memoir of Victory, Defeat, and Renewal* illustrates how someone may share the experiences of failure and at the same time work through all the emotions connected with that failure. On a recent talk show, Nixon explained this process and stated that life involves losing but that coping and never accepting defeat are the important things. While the scale of our failures may be different than his, the message is applicable to us all.

Remain Objective. In developing ideas for this chapter, I asked some colleagues what suggestions they might have for coping with failure. Mable Grimes of the University of Missouri Extension, Lincoln, offered the following observation: "Do not assume you are the total reason for whatever occurred. By remaining objective, one can better see what was done, how it was done, why it failed to work, and how one might do it differently the next time. Self-bashing will not enhance self-learning and does nothing but magnify the mistake and make one feel bad. . . . One must reflect on what one did the first time in a calm, rational, and nondefensive manner."

Donald Schön (1987), in his book *Educating the Reflective Practitioner*, encourages professionals to take the time to reflect purposefully on what is happening with a set of events, or with a program, or with some project that is at hand. Reflective thinking involves remaining objective. *Fostering Critical Reflection* (Mezirow and Associates, 1990) also offers a variety of techniques for developing skills in critical reflection. These techniques include such approaches as journal writing, metaphor analysis, and conceptual mapping.

Whatever the technique you use for reflective practice, recognizing personal biases and the influence of those biases on the interpretation of events is an important step in being able to remain objective. This is a tough thing to do, but time and distance from the event can make a difference in how objective one can be.

Exercise. This suggestion doesn't need a lot of elaboration since much has been said and written about the physical and mental benefits of exercising. I would only add that episodic exercise is of limited value, but regular exercise can help keep us on a more even keel so that failures do not represent major changes in our lives.

Exercise is one aspect of maintaining a balance in your life. Balance allows you to return to a stable point (that "even keel") after an event, such as a failure, has upset you. To achieve balance, each of us must develop the right mix of elements in our life—that is, a mix of individual activities, such as exercise, combined with family, work, and community activities. Finding this mix involves knowing and accepting ourselves. Thus, learning to say no and feeling okay about it are also part of developing balance. And balance includes the development of values by which we can judge ourselves and the things going on in our lives.

Volunteer or Help Someone. Helping someone else can be a potent elixir. Your action doesn't have to be big or formal or cost a lot of money (if any). Just the simple gesture of helping someone else may not only benefit that person but also help you to focus on something besides your own problems. Volunteer work puts things in perspective—fast. For me, this type of activity has to be somewhat different from the way in which I help others as an adult and continuing educator.

Be Nice to Yourself. Isen (1970) reported that for some individuals times of failure are also times for increasing self-rewards. I believe continuing educators are among those vast numbers of people in human service jobs who forget to be nice to themselves. We spend all our time thinking about and doing good things for other people through our programming efforts, and we forget that our own well-being is central to our ability to help others. Again, what you do doesn't have to be big or extravagant, but treating yourself to something special can be a great way to cope with failure and stress. Something as simple as having lunch in the park or buying that book of poetry you have wanted for a while can do the trick. It can also include activities that will enhance our abilities on the job but that we rarely seem to get around to: attending a faculty forum, calling a colleague, or reading a journal that would otherwise continue to gather dust.

Smile. The simple gesture of smiling can brighten your day and that of those around you. What does this have to do with coping with failure? Again, it keeps things in perspective. Negative thoughts breed negative thoughts; smiles breed smiles and friendly responses. An announcer on a local radio station here in Athens, Georgia, comments every morning, "Smile until 10:00 and the rest of the day will take care of itself!" That's probably stretching the truth just a bit, but it's the thought that counts. If you know of someone who is experiencing the impact of failure, extend a smile to that person. This is a good way to get sharing started.

Do Something Wacky—Break Routines. Whatever your habits, change something in your daily routine if only just for a day. If you never ever eat ice cream before noon, get an ice cream cone one morning. Take a mental health day and get away from it all. I wouldn't suggest this as a regular routine if you want to keep your job, but once in a while it can be good for you and those around you. Speak to someone you never speak to and see what happens. Wear something weird one day. The list goes on and on. The point is, break routine and *laugh* with yourself.

Read Something Inspirational. This may sound funny, but I like to read *Reader's Digest* for short, inspirational stories and quotes. Every issue has a story in it that reminds me of the fortitude of the human spirit. You may have a different favorite, but the point is that you have something to draw from for personal inspiration and growth. A helpful book to which I was recently introduced, for example, is *The Tao of Leadership* by John Heider (1990). Inspirational reading can also be incorporated in the techniques for sharing and reflective thinking.

Take a Risk on Another Program. All the analysis of the failure that you have done and the feedback that you have received can only help you be more successful on the next effort. Adult educators must surely view taking risks as part of their responsibility.

Recent articles in the popular press have focused on the fact that companies are beginning to reward risk takers. These companies are recognizing that you have to try out ideas—many of them—for successes to emerge, so they are creating environments where taking risks and talking about them are safe. Cocks (1990) underscored this by summarizing the trend toward creative problem solving and the fact that such problem solving involves taking risks and failing. There's nothing like getting busy on a new project to help us forget the misery of a previous one. By learning our lessons well and, we hope, at not too great an expense, we can take those failed experiences and make many more successes out of them.

Conclusion

Draw on these responses and others that you come up with when faced with failure. Only you can judge to what extent each response can be helpful for you and which response is appropriate for the occasion. Here's to successful failing!

References

Brookfield, S. D. "Using Critical Incidents to Explore Learners' Assumptions." In J. D. Mezirow and Associates, *Fostering Critical Reflection in Adulthood: A Guide to Transformative and Emancipatory Learning.* San Francisco: Jossey-Bass, 1990.

Campbell, R. "Overcoming Failure . . . After Failure . . . After Failure." *Woman's Day,* May 9, 1989, pp. 78-80.

Clifford, M. M. "Effects of Failure: Alternative Explanations and Possible Implications." *Educational Psychologist,* 1979, *14,* 44-52.

Cocks, J. "Let's Get Crazy." *Time,* June 11, 1990, 40-41.

Driscoll, D. "The Benefits of Failure." *Sales and Marketing Management,* 1989, *141,* 46-50.

Finesilver, S. G. "The Tapestry of Your Life: Don't be Afraid to Fail." *Vital Speeches of the Day,* 1989, *56,* 82-84.

Grogg, P. M. "On the Job: Dealing with Failure." *Working Woman*, 1983, *466*, 88, 90–91.

Heider, J. *The Tao of Leadership*. New York: Bantam Books, 1990.

Isen, A. M. "Success, Failure, Attention, and Recreation to Others: The Warm Glow of Success." *Journal of Personality and Social Psychology*, 1970, *15* (4), 294–301.

Keller, M. J., and Mills, H. H. "How Do You Feel After a Program Failure?" *Lifelong Learning: An Omnibus of Practice and Research*, 1983, *7* (3), 29–30.

Mezirow, J. D., and Associates. *Fostering Critical Reflection in Adulthood: A Guide to Transformative and Emancipatory Learning*. San Francisco: Jossey-Bass, 1990.

Nixon, R. M. *In the Arena: A Memoir of Victory, Defeat, and Renewal*. New York: Simon & Schuster, 1990.

Schön, D. A. *Educating the Reflective Practitioner: Toward a New Design for Teaching and Learning in the Professions*. San Francisco: Jossey-Bass, 1987.

Helen H. Mills is department head, Personal Adult Learning Services, Georgia Center for Continuing Education, at the University of Georgia, Athens.

What we learn through careful study of our mistakes gives us
powerful tools for planning.

Tools for Planning Better Programs

Thomas J. Sork

All of the chapters in this volume have addressed the topic of failures in the design and delivery of educational programs for adults. Although, in practice, failures like those discussed in these pages are not happy events, they provide important opportunities to develop a better understanding of what good planning entails.

The bulk of the literature on program planning consists of descriptions of how various authors think it "should be done" (Sork and Buskey, 1986). These descriptions are useful tools because they provide a way of thinking about and organizing the myriad decisions and tasks that are part of good planning. Yet some of the cases discussed in earlier chapters suggest that even when following a systematic planning model, failures occur. The careful analysis of mistakes made in the design and delivery of programs could be the basis for developing a much more powerful set of tools for planning—empirically grounded theoretical propositions about planning that are specific to the context in which they are generated. Put another way, by understanding what mistakes are most often made and how they can be corrected, we will be able to develop a much richer theory of planning than now exists. I have described this elsewhere as the process of building an inductively derived planning theory (Sork, 1986).

From Speculative Assertions to Principles of Practice

The literature contains many examples of speculative assertions about what "good" planning entails. Many of these can be stated in the following form: "If you wish to plan effective educational programs for adults, then you ought to x," where x is usually an action of some sort that is thought to be a characteristic of good planning. But what is often missing from this literature is a convincing rationale or some evidence to support the assertion. This leaves practitioners with only a few options. First, they can simply ignore the assertion. There is good evidence that many practitioners do just that, relying instead on their own experience and the advice of their colleagues. Second, they can assume the assertion is valid and change their practice to incorporate it. This is a bit risky, since the assertion may or may not be valid in the context where practitioners work. Third, they can test the validity of the assertion to see if it is valid where they work and only when they are convinced that it is will they change their practice to incorporate it.

Parry (1987) proposes twelve reasons why training programs fail in business and industrial settings. The twelve reasons he cites are (1) lack of support from top management, (2) little knowledge of audience and its needs, (3) inadequate preselling of participants by the bosses, (4) lack of instructor credibility or familiarity with subject, (5) too much lecture and one-way communication, (6) program is canned (the "not invented here" syndrome), (7) too much theory with no "how to" or "hands on," (8) the program drives a wedge between participant and boss, (9) no transfers of training from classroom to job, (10) wrong people as participants, (11) no evaluation of impact, and (12) no ongoing plan for continued growth. Each of these can be put into the general form of an assertion about good planning. For example, the first reason could be converted into the following assertion: "If you want your training programs to be successful, then getting the support of top management is crucial." Practitioners can reject this, accept it, or test it.

The several chapters in this volume that address specific types of failure also include speculations about what caused the failure and suggestions about how failure can be avoided. If these were thought of as hypotheses to be tested by you in the setting where you work, you could develop your own principles of practice based on what worked and what didn't.

To illustrate this process, I will use some of my own speculations about the likely causes of four types of planning and program failures. The definitions of these types of failure are taken from Sork, Kalef, and Worsfold (1987), and the list of possible causes is taken from Sork (1987). I should point out that it would be a rare failure that had only one cause. In Chapter Two, Lewis and Dunlop reported that when practitioners were asked why programs were unsuccessful, they invariably gave multiple reasons. This tells us that we should be suspicious if we or others conclude that a failure was caused by only one factor. Indeed, in most cases there is likely to be a causal chain—a string of interrelated events, decisions, and circumstances—that best explains the kinds of failures we are concerned with here.

Type 1 Failure. Planning for the program is partially completed but is terminated before implementation. Organizational resources are expended on planning with the full intention of offering a program, but for some reason a decision is made to terminate planning. Possible causes include:

Agency goals or mandate not clear
Client systems not well defined
No consensus on focus of program
Incomplete knowledge of resource constraints
Responsibilities of those involved not defined
Tentative design too costly
Tentative design too complex
Lack of follow-through.

Type 2 Failure. Planning for the program is completed and the offering is publicized, but it does not attract sufficient enrollments or registrations and is therefore canceled. Possible causes include:

Inappropriate pricing
Inappropriate scheduling
Inappropriate location
Not of interest to client group
Poorly focused promotion
Poorly timed promotion
Competition more attractive
Market saturation
Inadequate support services
Mismatch between agency and program.

Type 3 Failure. Planning for the program is completed, the offering is publicized, and enough people enroll so the program is offered. But the program does not provide what the participants had expected, so they either fail to complete the program (drop out) or react so negatively to it that no consideration is given to offering the program again in its original form. Possible causes include:

Poor instructor
Poor administration
Unclear objectives
Mismatch between content and client needs
Too elementary
Too advanced
Inappropriate instructional methods
Poor quality of noninstructional resources
Misleading advertising.

Type 4 Failure. The program is offered and the participants express satisfaction, but there is clear evidence that the program failed to achieve the objectives for which it was designed. Although some useful learning may have been a consequence of the program and may account for the satisfaction expressed by the participants, the learning does not correspond to the objectives of the program. Possible causes include:

Ineffective instruction
Unclear objectives
Miscommunication of objectives
Too many objectives
Unrealistic expectations
Mismatch between objectives and instructional methods
Inadequate provision for transfer of learning.

Translating Causes into Principles. Let's begin with the first cause of Type 1 failures—agency goals or mandate not clear. Before deciding what action to take to eliminate this cause, we must go through several steps to reason our way to a promising hypothesis. First we must be convinced that unclear goals or mandate is a factor in the causal chain that explains the failure. To be convinced, we must think carefully about the events leading up to the termination of planning. If, on reflection, we find that we devoted resources to planning because we thought that the program idea was within the mandate of our agency but, when discussing our activities with our supervisor, we found that he or she did not consider the idea at all relevant to the agency's goals or mandate, we have evidence that this factor may have been part of the chain. Before concluding that it is, we must first explore a bit more. We must determine whether the mandate is not clear or whether we simply did not understand the mandate.

Whether the mandate is clearly articulated and available to those in the agency is one thing, but whether we or others in the agency are aware of and understand it is quite another. For purposes of this analysis, we will assume that the mandate has not been clarified, so those who design programs have developed different views of what the mandate is. If we are concerned about the resources that are "wasted" due to this type of failure, then we may propose that the agency take steps to clarify its mandate and make sure that everyone understands it. Now we are able to generate a hypothesis that can be tested in practice. The hypothesis might sound something like this: "If the agency clarifies its mandate and ensures that all programmers understand what the mandate is and how it should be applied to assess the relevance of program ideas, then there will be a reduction in Type 1 failures." Remember that this is only a hypothesis—a speculative assertion—that remains to be tested. The mandate could then be clarified and programmers briefed on how to use it to assess program ideas. Then, if there is a drop in the incidence of Type 1 failures, the hypothesis would be supported, and we would have increased confidence in its validity. If support for the hypothesis is found in other agencies, then our confidence in it continues to increase to the point where we stop viewing it as a hypothesis and begin viewing it as a principle of practice.

Let's work through one more example, this time from the list of causes of Type 2 failures. The first item in that list is inappropriate pricing. For this analysis we will assume that through a bit of follow-up work we found that the most frequently mentioned reason for not registering was "fee too high." From research on participation we know that potential attendees' *ability* to pay and their *willingness* to pay are two different dimensions of the problem of nonparticipation. Now we have the basis for a hypothesis that might look something like this: "If fees are established by taking into account not only the costs of offering the program but also the ability and willingness of the potential participants to pay the fees, then there will be a decrease in Type 2 failures." As in the first example, if we test this hypothesis and gain confidence in its validity, its status changes from a speculative assertion to a principle of practice.

From Principles of Practice to Planning Theory

The examples provided here could be repeated for each of the causes listed in this chapter and throughout the volume, resulting in dozens of hypotheses. These, in turn, could lead to dozens of principles of practice that, when taken together and related to one another, will become planning theory. Whether we realize it or not, we all employ personal theories of planning that are based on what has been shown to work for others, what has worked for us, or what we expect will work in a given circumstance. Our personal planning theories are constantly being tested and revised in practice. Every time we do things that work, our theories are reinforced, and every time we do things that don't work, our theories are challenged. If we believe that our theories are flawed, we usually revise them and then change our practice accordingly.

Before we introduce a new principle into our theory of practice, it is wise to test the validity of the proposition in the context of our work. The suggestions for reducing the incidence of failure presented in this volume have been more or less validated in contexts familiar to the authors. Readers seeing the merits of adopting these suggestions are encouraged to test them in their own context and, if the suggestions work, to incorporate them into practice. Adopting this approach to developing personally relevant and empirically validated planning theory takes energy and a commitment to reflective practice. But it is through such work that more sophisticated planning theory will be developed, and this is a prerequisite of more sophisticated practice.

Conclusion

There are compelling practical reasons for being concerned about failure in adult and continuing education and for taking action to reduce it. The monetary and nonmonetary costs of failure can be substantial. This volume has focused attention on the mistakes that we make in the design and delivery of educational programs for adults and the lessons that can be learned from those mistakes. It has introduced new research findings about how practitioners regard failure and what factors they believe most often account for failure. Four different types of failures have been discussed in detail; those resulting in insufficient participation, negative reactions to programs, little or no intended learning, and lack of transfer to the natural environment. Possible responses to failure have also been addressed.

Ten years ago when I first wrote about failure in adult and continuing education (Sork, 1981), I expressed the hope that more people would take up the challenge to analyze their failures systematically and publish their conclusions as Smith (1974, 1975) and Lewis and Fockler (1976) had done. As yet, with the exception of Hanson (1982), that hope is unfulfilled. Doing the analysis and keeping the results private may have personal or organizational benefits, but it is only through publication of such analyses that other practitioners and the profession can benefit. Now I hope that this volume will stimulate its readers to recognize failure as a natural part of adult and continuing education practice, to learn as much as possible from their mistakes, and to share those lessons with others through publication.

References

Hanson, A. L. "Anatomy of a Canceled Continuing Education Program." *American Journal of Pharmaceutical Education*, 1982, 46 (1), 23–27.

Lewis, T. G., and Fockler, M. E. "Help! My Training Program Bombed . . . and It Could Happen to Yours!" *Training*, 1976, 13 (6), 26–27, 30.

Parry, S. *Reasons Why Training Programs Succeed or Fail.* Princeton, N.J.: Training House, 1987.

Smith, R. M. "A Case Study of a Programming Failure." *Adult Leadership*, 1974, 22 (8), 266, 284.

Smith, R. M. "A Case Study: No One for Puerto Rico." *Adult Leadership*, 1975, 23 (11), 322, 330.

Sork, T. J. "The Postmortem Audit: Improving Programs by Examining 'Failures.'" *Lifelong Learning: The Adult Years*, 1981, 5 (3), 6–7, 31.

Sork, T. J. "The Postmortem Audit: A Research Methodology for Building Inductively Derived Planning Theory." *Proceedings of the 27th Annual Adult Education Research Conference.* Syracuse, N.Y.: Syracuse University, 1986.

Sork, T. J. "Toward a Causal Model of Program Failure in Adult Education." *Proceedings of the 28th Annual Adult Education Research Conference.* Laramie: University of Wyoming, 1987.

Sork, T. J., and Buskey, J. H. "A Descriptive and Evaluative Analysis of Program Planning Literature, 1950-1983." *Adult Education Quarterly,* 1986, *36* (2), 86-96.

Sork, T. J., Kalef, R., and Worsfold, N. E. *The Postmortem Audit: A Strategy for Improving Educational Programs.* Vancouver, British Columbia, Canada: Intentional Learning Systems, 1987.

Thomas J. Sork is associate professor of adult education at the University of British Columbia.

INDEX

Ordering Information

New Directions for Adult and Continuing Education is a series of paperback books that explores issues of common interest to instructors, administrators, counselors, and policy makers in a broad range of adult and continuing education settings—such as colleges and universities, extension programs, businesses, the military, prisons, libraries, and museums. Books in the series are published quarterly in Fall, Winter, Spring, and Summer and are available for purchase by subscription as well as by single copy.

Subscriptions for 1991 cost $45.00 for individuals (a savings of 20 percent over single-copy prices) and $60.00 for institutions, agencies, and libraries. Please do not send institutional checks for personal subscriptions. Standing orders are accepted.

Single copies cost $13.95 when payment accompanies order. (California, New Jersey, New York, and Washington, D.C., residents please include appropriate sales tax.) Billed orders will be charged postage and handling.

Discounts for quantity orders are available. Please write to the address below for information.

All orders must include either the name of an individual or an official purchase order number. Please submit your order as follows:
  Subscriptions: specify series and year subscription is to begin
  Single copies: include individual title code (such as CE1)

Mail all orders to:
  Jossey-Bass Inc., Publishers
  350 Sansome Street
  San Francisco, California 94104

For sales outside of the United States contact:
  Maxwell Macmillan International Publishing Group
  866 Third Avenue
  New York, New York 10022